# PRINCIPLES of
# SOCIAL CASE RECORDING

# PRINCIPLES *of* SOCIAL CASE RECORDING

By GORDON HAMILTON

PUBLISHED FOR
THE NEW YORK SCHOOL OF SOCIAL WORK
BY COLUMBIA UNIVERSITY PRESS
NEW YORK

## PREFACE

WHEN ABOUT TEN YEARS AGO I PUBLISHED A SMALL book on Social Case Recording, I was hesitant to state principles definitely lest rigidity or stereotyping should result. Now, after many years as a student of case recording in all fields, while still aware of the danger of a model record, I have come to believe that the main princip'es of good case recording can be helpfully formulated. Although in this ten-year period there have been some striking changes in case work practice, I have not found the principles of recording altered. It is true that in 1935 and 1936 the recording of process was in high favor, while today, summary, selection, diagnosis, and evaluation are receiving most attention, as might be expected with professional growth and the deepening and control of professional thinking. But swings of fashion will always occur without changing the main disciplines of professional writing. In the present edition, I have stated several basic principles through the device of chapter headings, and more fully in a summary of each chapter. Although I have addressed myself to the science and art of recording and not of case work, as such, I have been at great pains to discuss and illustrate practices which reflect the more important contemporary trends, so that I hope the student of case work will be helped to grasp more fully the dynamics of the case work process itself. I have not attempted to review the rules of English composition, a minimum familiarity with which improves any writing! He who does not already write with logic and clarity will never learn excellence through case recording. The essence of case recording is primarily content, only secondarily structure and style.

To reproduce enough of a case record to show clearly the direction of study or treatment or helping is of course impractical, and we must assume that it is not relevant to argue from small cross-sections arbitrarily lifted out of context whether or not the case work is valid, or indeed whether it demonstrates any special emphasis or approach. Rather, we must ask, is this a good way to describe a social situation or the use of relationship? What kinds of summaries should be introduced? Is this what is meant by case work diagnosis or evaluation? What makes for a good professional style? All the illustrations are disguised, and I have usually reduced or omitted identifying data rather than made artificial substitutions. otherwise editing is minimal. The purpose is to give real and useful rather than model examples.

The illustrations are taken for convenience from one urban center. As a student of records in many cities, I have not found differences which would suggest regional styles, and I find this encouraging as a mark of an established profession. Differences in rural recording, whenever skilled practitioners are employed, are also minor. I have included illustrations of what is popularly called the "functional" approach, but I have not attempted to show how differences in approach may condition recording because the effect, I believe, is upon total contents and direction rather than upon component processes, which remain constant.

Throughout the first seven chapters, examples drawn from a range of fields have been freely and interchangeably used for their general applicability. That records must be adapted to agency purpose and function as well as to the individual case is now so generally accepted that one need only reaffirm it as a principle. Although I believe it is less useful to have a compendium on recording in all fields than to recognize the basic forms and elements of the process, I have, in Chapter 8, discussed certain special emphases in a few fields. The student, however, is cautioned that he cannot understand the peculiar problems of any agency or field without a thorough knowledge of general recording.

My most grateful acknowledgments go not only to those workers and students who have so generously given of their own creative work, but to agencies and institutions which have permitted the use of material, both in this and in earlier editions.

I wish to acknowledge additional contributions from the Children's Aid Society, the Community Service Society, Family Service, the Department of Welfare, the Children's Court, the Bureau of Child Guidance of the Board of Education, the Jewish Social Service Association, the Jewish Family Welfare Society, the Jewish Board of Guardians, the New York Association of Jewish Children, the Presbyterian Hospital, and the New York State Psychiatric Institute, all of New York City; and from the Department of Child Welfare of Westchester County.

I am also greatly indebted to various members of the faculty of the New York School of Social Work, Columbia University, and to Miss Jean Kallenberg, Miss Florence Harvey, Mrs. Helen Perlman, for reading parts of the manuscript, and especially to Miss Anna Kempshall, for her professional criticism and advice; to Miss Mabel P. Ashley for editorial assistance, and to Miss Carol White for her preparation of the manuscript.

G. H.

*New York*
*August, 1945*

# CONTENTS

# 1

## RECORDING AND PRACTICE ARE INTER-DEPENDENT AND INTERRELATED

A BOOK ON SOCIAL CASE RECORDING SHOULD, PERHAPS, begin with a short discussion of the practice which is to be recorded. There is some natural correspondence between the contents of practice itself and the form used to demonstrate it, although it is also true that the same contents may be written up in several ways. Conditioned as practice is by agency requirements, the basic methods remain common to all types of case work. So too recording—sometimes flexibly, sometimes routinely adapted to the agency program—has common purposes and disciplines. We shall do well, then, to examine some of the characteristics of social case work which become the essential elements of the problem of recording.

Social case work has always proved elusive in definition, because the social sciences and civilization are themselves fluid and elusive. The social order is a scheme of relationship which the social sciences are particularly charged with studying and understanding. Social work as a profession is concerned not only with the adjustments of people within a social order but with contributing to changes in the social order, since one of the known facts of science seems to be that human relations are not permanently and irrevocably fixed. Social work is concerned with the adaptation of person to person, person to group, person to situation, and inter-group relations, and these constellations may shift from century to century and from culture to culture. Early concepts of welfare were expressed largely in such terms as "charities" and "corrections"—that is to say, food, shelter, and clothing for the poor, and reform for the ill-doer. But these concepts have been steadily broadening to include positive health and welfare for all people, and deepening to the objectives of guidance and prevention and social planning in the field of behavior, as well as economic problems.

To the social worker an adequate standard of living means not only economic subsistence but opportunities for development and social contribution. As the political scientist Charles E. Merriam once put it, "there must be adequate distribution of civilization's gains." Social work today finds its objective in furthering the more adequate distribution of civilization's gains, and as the coverage increases we find social work no longer addressing itself exclusively to the needs of the poor, but to the needs, adjustments, and adaptations of human beings in a wide range of social situations. The social case worker has had to learn that social adaptation is a complex reaction. Sometimes the failure to adapt may be seen as an external clash between the individual and his environment. This is a "primary" form of unadjustment. But more often the failure to adjust derives from a combination of internal strain and external pressure. Always the person's attitude towards his situation, his emotional involvement, must be considered as part of the situation itself. People not only are in situations, they create situations. The case worker, therefore, is educated to understand not only the external objective facts in a social situation, but the person's behavior towards his situation, his feelings about himself in his situation.

The implications for case recording are obvious. The task of reproducing and analyzing this dynamic configuration of person-situation is very difficult. Closely related to this is another case work assumption. Social case work would be a relatively simple art if we conceived of the client as a passive recipient of a program of commodities and services. But the democratic hypothesis of representative government has its counterpart in representative welfare; that is to say, the individual, group, and community are not only participants, but chief participants, in the resolution of their own affairs. The case worker, therefore, is typically engaged in a shared enterprise, his ability to be of service depending on his skilled ability to relate himself constructively to a person in a complex and fluid situation. Giving a commodity to a person or imposing a service is one thing, helping a person to use a resource or a service and to use a case work relationship toward self-development is another. To translate this second process into a record is quite difficult.

· REASONS FOR RECORDING

Why, then, do we record at all? Because to practice, no matter how conscientiously, is never enough. The practitioner in any one of the humanitarian professions is obligated to improve his skill in the interest of his clients, and to make his profession as a whole increasingly effective in the public interest. The subject matter of his profession must be communicable so that each new worker does not have to learn by trial and error. The practitioner must be constantly student and critic of what he does, and there is no one way more likely to make us think than to have to write out our reflections. Nothing is more likely to help the quality of performance than a careful accounting of this performance. A first essential in improving case work service to clients is to acquire the habit of careful observation and accurate written description. The next essential is to learn to analyze and interpret the data, and to record one's thinking in the case record. It would be fair to say that all first-rate practitioners are impatient with the time spent on the case record, but none would eliminate it. They know too well from experience how indispensable the case record is for the protection of the client, for the development of skill, and for the building up of new knowledge. Moreover, the fact that all social case work is practiced in agencies and that there is considerable mobility and turnover in most staffs makes a responsible shared account invaluable.[1]

[1]A good way to improve one's practice is to study not only one's own records but those of representative agencies. Fortunately today there is considerable "full-length" material available. The earliest collections of case material, those records dating back to 1902, prepared in 1911 by Mary Richmond for the Russell Sage Foundation and privately printed are now, unfortunately, out of print, as are the Judge Baker Foundation series of about a decade later. The University of Chicago Press has done the field the service of printing case books from time to time. Jour-

The purposes of keeping social case records have been adequately described by Sheffield, Bristol,[2] and others, and need no further elaboration here. These purposes are usually formulated as practice, administration, teaching, and research. Linked as these purposes are, the dominant consideration, which is the focus of this book, is that of practice, that is, of service to clients. In most colleges the student is individualized by ratings, grades, and descriptive material. In medical and psychological institutions, charts, photographs, and graphs supplement and almost replace the written word. In the social services, although experiments continue to try to isolate measurable units which can be classified and standardized, and from which predictions and generalizations may be made, reliable tests, useful in social work, have not yet been much developed. On the other hand, the interviewing process in skilled hands has become a highly sensitive instrument. The social case record of today, though it makes use of documentary sources, of tests, reports, and measurements from other fields, derives its peculiar characteristics from the direct observation of social setting and behavior, and from the central place given to the interviewing process.

The most important thing about a professional record lies in its contents. Although good practice is not necessarily reflected by good recording, there is a natural interplay between knowing what one is doing and reporting well what one has been doing. The chief function of the record is to show the nature of the case situation, what the client is doing about his problem, and how case workers carry the responsibility of offering help or treatment. The nature of the social case itself is so complex and fluid that the various factors must be carefully described. Social

---

nals such as *The Family*, and the publications of the various schools of social work, give excellent pictures of cases *in extenso*. Case record exhibits of the Family Welfare Association of America, and the Child Welfare League of America have done much to familiarize the student with the total case. Volumes of the *Journal of Social Work Process* give illustrations of process in the so-called "functional" approach in which eligibility for the agency service is regarded as the chief dynamic of movement and change.

[2] See Ada E. Sheffield, *Social Case History; Its Construction and Content*, and Margaret C. Bristol, *Handbook on Social Case Recording*.

situations are not easily stated, still less recaptured; it is impossible to carry a great quantity of case details in one's head; and since social work is typically organized within agencies and institutions rather than in private practice, the group or team use of a record makes lucid, concise, and accurate recording indispensable. In spite of the need which most of us have to find rules and absolute procedures to guide us, at the outset one must face the fact that there is no such thing as a model record; there are no routines which will make the case inevitably clear, accessible, and understandable. Records should be written to suit the case, not the case geared to a theoretical pattern. There are no canons of mass or coherence, no dramatic unities to which the living human situation can be shaped. True, unity of a sort is achieved through the development of social case work as a consciously controlled method, but each case still is different, the conditions of work hold marked differences, and the recording, therefore, rests not on the following of an outline, but on the *mastery of certain component processes*. Given these, the case worker decides what data are needed, what structure and style best suit the material and reveal its significances. These contents, then, become the medium through which the worker in the agency and his associates may keep accurate track of the developments in the case, and also deepen their understanding and improve their skill.

We shall not describe in detail the administrative purpose of records. The case record serves as an administrative tool, as it is the chief source of information in determining need for assistance.[3] It is often an index to the necessity for correction of policies or ineffective practices; it helps in the adjudication of complaints and tends to improve the quality of service. As social situations change, the case record is important for an analysis and clarification of services. Changes in staff also make the continuity of the case records necessary.

In earlier days the case record was a sort of omnibus affair designed not only to show what was done *for* the client, but to show effort, "production," business transactions, appointments,

[3]See p. 97.

and other administrative concerns now properly kept elsewhere. The trend has been to relieve the case record of bookkeeping, bill collecting, and other financial transactions; the number of visits, or telephone calls made, or letters written; and to transfer these and other kinds of case accounting to appropriate reports and indices. Readers interested in these secondary forms of recording may consult several useful texts[4] and pamphlets. Administrative reporting and accounting is typically done through ledger cards, statistical sheets, and other standard forms; *discussion* of administrative policies and procedures with the client, however, is an important part of the case history. Thus, authorizations, vouchers, and the issuance of grants are kept in the "business" part of the office; interviews with the client about eligibility, budgeting, board rates or amount and kind of assistance are appropriate material for the case history.[5] The use of structure and function in the case work process belongs in the narrative, the mechanics do not.

We cannot here devote attention to the uses of records for research or classroom teaching, although the record is an important tool in student supervision. If and when dictaphonic records are widely developed for classroom and supervisory use there will be less pressure on the case record for extremely detailed observations. The student new to field work is encouraged to write in longhand careful notes of all that goes on between himself and the client, and all contacts with the community. At first he sees little, and that little inaccurately; he is even less able to record the significance of his observations and interviews. As knowledge and skill develop he becomes able to report with clarity and precision, then to select and condense in summary, and finally to embark on the adventure of interpretation, of recording his own social judgments on observed phenomena. The novice is not likely to achieve a short, well-selected record until he has been taught to produce a thoughtful, complete one. Training in the writing of narrative, summary, and diagnosis should proceed

[4]See Mary A. Clark, *Recording and Reporting for Child Guidance Clinics;* H. I. Fisk, *Statistical Recording and Reporting in Family Welfare Agencies; Social Case Histories of Public Assistance Agencies*, Social Security Board.
[5]See Chapter 8 for discussion of public assistance records.

at the same time, though not always at the same pace, and the stages of development for the average student are approximately in the order given. Any first-year student should have made a substantial beginning in all three aspects of case recording.

Research studies should be planned in advance whenever possible, since the ex post facto recourse to data can afford only limited results. The social worker not only has the responsibility of obtaining pertinent facts for use in planning with individuals for the treatment best suited to his particular situation, but for assembling data which may lead to fresh knowledge about the nature of social problems and community needs, as well as analysis of social treatment itself—its successes and failures. Criteria for success and failure, for case movement, still largely elude us. A satisfactory classification of problems has yet to be devised, or any agreement on what is meant in social work by improvement or adjustment. Social workers are still forced to use common sense rather than "scientific" judgments as to the reduction of, or better balance of, external pressures and internal strains. In successful instances case workers record in their closing entries that a man is employed instead of unemployed, well instead of ailing, better fed or housed or with better wages; and also that the parent has stopped nagging the child, or the child his truanting or ganging; or more subtle but no less important evidence to show that the person is more comfortable within himself, less tense or anxious or irritable, more secure in his social relations. Likewise in unsuccessful cases, one must face and learn from one's mistakes, and so improve the quality of service to clients. When young workers begin to want to study their own records with a supervisor or with a group, and have become relatively undefensive about discussing their efforts and failures, one can say that they are really maturing as professional persons.

Every responsible worker has two records—his notebook and the agency record. Recording will never improve if the worker keeps everything of significance in his notebook and commits only routine items and events to the permanent record. Nor will it improve if the worker dictates everything that happened in the most trivial conversation to the patient dictaphone. Recording improves when the worker writes full observations in a well-kept notebook, reviews these notes and selects therefrom significant verbal data, behavior, events, and his own thinking for dictation to the agency document.

"Reading maketh a full man, conference a ready man, and writing an exact man," said Bacon. Unfortunately, as knowledge of a subject grows, it is hard for the writer of a journal or record to retain simplicity as well as truth. The case worker is nothing if he has not a broad human view based on close and, one may say, loving interest in the drama of existence. The case worker who is not curious about people and concerned about helping them will never be a great case worker, but his professional discipline is yet "to abstain, to distinguish, to prefer," recognizing the limitations, not of the life experience, which can have no exact boundaries, but of his own role. This is just as true of recording. To workers who say anxiously, "Should we not put in everything in the event that some of it later may prove important?" the answer is that we should study again and again, not merely complicated situations but the obvious and the dull, to be sure that significance has not eluded us, and that what we see is really our business. After such sifting, what we then choose as probably relevant belongs in the case record. Effective recording, like effective listening, is always an active process of attention and selection. "It is not the recording," as a wise case worker once said, "which is difficult; it is the thinking which precedes it." If we can think clearly about the client's needs, his circumstances, and the treatment or movement, the record will shape itself easily and simply.

· *SUMMARY*

The purposes of a case record are those of: practice, to ensure adequate service to the client; administration, to review and evaluate the discharge of this responsibility; teaching and supervision, to communicate knowledge and improve skill; and research, to discover new knowledge and to assist in social planning and prevention. Records are for professional use, and their contents are of first importance. Training in the stuff-of-life experience and learning what the client and ourselves can do together to help him must be the basis of achievement of skill in recording. Or, even more truly, it may be said that discipline in case recording is one of the most important devices now known in developing skill in case work.

Ideally, the record is intended to project our observations and findings; to help us check on our observations; to show our relationship to our clients; our role in helping them; to aid us in formulating our hypotheses and to appraise movement, change, growth, or negative and unsuccessful treatment. Responsible practice requires a careful record, but quality of service is improved by the use of records for supervision and other forms of teaching. Records, especially if the problems to be solved are laid down in advance, are extremely important in research. Research is an obligation not yet widely enough assumed to affect current trends in case recording. It can only be hoped that substantial case work studies will have the effect of producing more comparable, measurable data, develop a more reliable terminology, and through standardized testing devices permit more understanding of the meaning of success and the causes of failure. The structure and function of an agency impose certain administrative necessities, but the more mechanical aids to administration find their expression in supplementary cards and reports rather than in the case record.

## 2

## RECORDS ARE FOR USE

ONE OF THE REASONS WHY STUDENTS, YOUNG WORKERS, and such administrators as have never themselves practiced case work show a resistance to case recording is that they do not visualize clearly the use of records in treatment. "I don't want to be bothered with all that writing," says the layman; "Recording is an interruption to case work," says a beginner in social work. If it were a banking process they would understand why accounts must be kept, or in a factory they would raise no question about proper records and reports, but when it is "just" people and their concerns they can see no reason for keeping track of these. Case workers know from experience that they do have to keep track of the difficult aspects of human experience —clients reacting to their social situation, and to those who are trying to help them. Case workers have learned that it is just as poor economy not to have adequate records of social facts, attitudes, and behavior in the case work transaction as in the business transaction.

Records are for professional use. They are not created as a form of literature; they are not created for aesthetic enjoyment, nor are they made to be laid away in a file. They are designed to help the worker in a realistic, practical way, to serve the client's interest, and to further social work knowledge in the interest of the next client. For most efficient use we must then consider format, structure, arrangement, contents, and style. Obviously, contents are the most important; but contents, no matter how valuable, if inaccessible because of physical arrangement or endless repetition or obscurities of style, are useless.

### · FORMAT, STRUCTURE, ARRANGEMENT

Format, structure, arrangement should contribute to usefulness. Since records are repeatedly handled they should be strongly bound and conveniently arranged, with all materials organized for visibility and readability. At the beginning of the century records were less convenient, often hand written, or on half sheets of paper loosely clipped together, or worse still, folded and placed in an envelope. They were not designed for ready reference. The origin of the phrase "red tape" is sometimes ascribed to the Civil War veterans' records which were placed in envelopes and tied with yards of tape cumbersome to deal with. Since a number of workers in an agency are likely to read a record either concurrently or in succession, one may assert reasonably that the time cost in using a record is always more of a consideration than the time cost in organizing, dictating, and transcribing it, so that care spent in preparation is always cheap in the long run.

The physical characteristics of the average modern record are as follows: bound in a manilla or slightly heavier paper folder, firmly held together at the left-hand margin, by one of several reliable devices, the record opens flat like a book and reads from left to right. Correspondence may be either inter-leaved or filed chronologically at the back. On the outside of the folder,[1] the administrative status of the case—for example, "open," "closed," with dates—may be stamped, the name and number on the upper edge or tab. Records should be typed, have comfortable margins, some index headings, and a reasonable amount of paragraphing. An unbroken single-spaced page, while saving of paper, is hard on the eye. The ordinary rules for paragraphing are not entirely relevant to the professional record because material derived from clients is discontinuous and illogical, and, as Gertrude Stein once said in a lecture on Narration: "Paragraphing is a thing that anyone is enjoying and sentences are less fascinating but then . gradually you find that it is not really necessary that everything has a beginning a middle and an ending. . ." Of course the case work process *has* a beginning, a

[1] Eva Abramson, *The Supervisor's Job in the Public Agency: Administrative Aspects.*

middle, and an ending, and the record in hard outline is responsive to this, but within this framework the themes cannot be too nicely set apart without violence to the truth of the experience itself.

## The Unit Record

The Unit Record is preferred whenever possible to a series of folders. [2] In earlier stages of social work various services were departmentalized, each department keeping its own record of the same client. In an agency today, in which case work is the recognized method of using *all* services, the case work process is integrated and the "unit" record developed. Thus, in public assistance when economic aid is conceived of as the central professional service, this theme becomes the main subject of the unified record. The appropriate consulting departments then, such as resource adjustment, home economics, settlement, and so forth, do not set up independent case record systems, but subserve or promote the main function by notations in the unit record. This would not preclude the consulting technical experts from keeping supplementary records, usually of a card file type, for the data needed for their specialties—arrangements for medical care or work placements, or the like. Likewise, in a child guidance agency, social worker, psychiatrist, and psychologist all contribute to the same record. Even when the case is divided, with one worker seeing the parent and one the child, or one the husband and another the wife, this does not usually require two separate charts because of the interaction of the persons concerned. Generally speaking, the unit record is not only physically unified, but it is like a novel about a family. The patient is not a biological unit, but by hypothesis a social unit, and the record an interpersonal one. We shall speak of this as a special problem of certain fields; for instance, medical-social and child placing, in a later chapter. [3]

Other types of agencies may have departmentalized bureaus within their framework (visiting nursing, visiting housekeeping,

[2]For the special problems of the child placing record, see Chapter 8.
[3]See Chapter 8.

home economics, business- or vocational-guidance services), the records of which must be combined. If departments are physically inaccessible, so that each must keep a complete record, it seems to be more satisfactory to exchange carbons at intervals than to prepare summaries which are never ready when the department wants them. But this amounts to the duplication of records, which is always somewhat unsatisfactory. If departments preserve their identities to this extent, we have an "assembled" and not precisely a "unit" record, and one must wonder if the case work process is itself integrated. If the departments are physically accessible, the entries of a visiting housekeeper or consultant may be interspersed chronologically among the entries of the case workers or others. Many child-placing records which at first glance appear departmentalized are textually integrated. On the whole it is best to construct a unit record with the necessary library facilities for circulation among the departments concerned. Indexing, the use of colored sheets for special summaries, and other devices, serve to articulate the several parts in the unit record.

Most records contain a face sheet,[4] history or narrative sheets, and correspondence, with special outlines or forms for budget, health, placement, and other data, as needed. Administrative forms and outlines, such as authorization vouchers, referral slips, interdepartmental memoranda, ledger cards, etc., should be omitted from the case record and kept in appropriate files and cabinets. Sometimes a copy of the latest authorizations may be retained in the folder for the current period until replaced. The "index of effort" and "overhead" items, telephone calls, number of appointments, need not be kept in the case record in "behold-me-busy" entries, but may be efficiently recorded on day sheets or other accounting devices. Records are then freed to serve their primary purpose.

## Face Sheet and Other Outlines

The face sheet or card shows the make-up of the family group. It has the purpose of giving identifying data about the persons

[4]Standard face sheets may be obtained from the Family Welfare Association of America, Child Welfare League of America, and other national or Federal agencies.

most concerned in the social situation. Names, addresses, occupations, relatives, citizenship, nationality, religion, birth and marriage dates, social status (that is, whether single, married, or divorced), distinguish this particular person and this family from others of the same name. A secondary purpose, also locating and identifying, is shown on face cards under such headings as "ward" or "clinic," "district," "precinct," "social worker," which tend to locate the family administratively in the agency rather than in society at large. Some people say that the face card should outline "the social situation at a glance." Rather, the face card should give in convenient form certain objective social facts of a more or less permanent character which particularize this case. In the course of a lifetime, one is frequently registered. It is wise not to place intimate facts or subtle or ephemeral material on a face card. The card should be so arranged as to permit several changes of address, or of school, or place of employment without making a fresh card at short intervals. Although a face sheet may be the basis of agency statistics, a card index is employed in most agencies, and this becomes the central file for subsequent identifications.

Face sheets should be simple, accurate, and up to date. They should, at a minimum, contain enough data to clear through a social service exchange. A maximum is harder to state, but nothing should be on a face sheet which is not likely to be used for ready reference. Administrative identifying data will vary with the function of the agency. In child placing work, the last address of the child and responsible guardian *must* be currently registered. The names and addresses of more than one relative are convenient as a means of locating families which move frequently. It is no longer thought necessary to put medical diagnoses or intelligence ratings on the face sheet. It is better for such material to go on a separate page or in the text with enough interpretation to make the classification useful. Social diagnoses are inherently too long to be placed on the face sheet and should be in the text. Social service exchange clearings may be typed on the face sheet or on the history sheet or, better still, stapled to the folder. In international case work, as with displaced persons, additional data dealing with nationality and migration status will be needed.

In agencies which use an application blank there may be duplication among the data on the blank, the face sheet, and the index card. Care should be taken to have no more overlapping forms than are absolutely indispensable, and to arrange identical material uniformly on supplementary blanks so as to facilitate copying. When workers are untrained and administrators unfamiliar with the process there is a tendency to the prolification of forms and outlines. This makes for greater inaccuracy than if a few essential, well-designed forms are used. Even so, there is legitimate range among agencies as to the kind and number of forms and outlines employed. Public agencies tend to the use of forms for such data as can and should be standardized. In fact, whenever data can be standardized a form may prove convenient. Unfortunately, the official mind also tends to preserve documents without regard to their permanent value. Thus, we often see in recurrent cases a series of reduplicating application forms which should have been removed after the new application[5] has been filed.

Outlines for social study are rarely printed on the history sheet, but such guides should be kept "under the blotter." Eligibility studies in public assistance may follow to some extent a predetermined pattern, as may histories for child guidance clinics, but even so, some flexibility is desirable. As a training in formal social study, outlines have a value, but it is always a temptation to fill in forms whether the material sought is pertinent or not. At one period workers were encouraged to get all the information possible and place it in the record on the chance that later some of it might prove to be significant; the present day worker is better trained to sift his material at the time. It is true, however, that the case records of the later years have become much less schematic and dependent on outlines, as if in response to a case work technique more controlled but less or-

[5]In rare instances old application blanks might be of sufficient interest for preservation, but that the application blank is likely to be the legal basis for prosecution is one of those curiously persistent myths, related to the obsolescent pauper's oath. Client signatures are also kept in a more convenient form today

ganized and organizing. It is probably true that as skill in diagnostic thinking has increased, reliance on schedules and outlines
for either history or analysis has lessened. In most agencies the
text consists of a succession of chronological entries broken by
summaries and interpretive writing. Summaries long banished
in favor of "process" are coming in again, and the really sophisticated record shows a balance between narrative and summarized writing.

## Correspondence

The only letters[6] which should be filed in the case record are
those to or about the client. Other correspondence belongs in
the business part of the office. Letters which relate to the treatment of the client may be interleaved with the text or else filed
consecutively at the end of the record, the latter procedure being
preferred by most agencies. Whether filed at the back or inter-
leaved, the text should include a dated entry as to the nature of
the letter, that is, "Letter received from John Smith about Pat-
rick's classroom problems," rather than merely, "Letter received." The entry should not be more than a line or two, since
for details the reader should consult the correspondence itself.
In agencies whose main function is correspondence, the letters
themselves may constitute the text.

Significant correspondence should be distinguished from insignificant in order not to clutter the text. Christmas greeting
cards, duplicates of letters—that is, returned original or carbons
—letters giving appointments, and interoffice administrative
communications should usually be weeded out and placed in
the wastepaper basket. Great care, however, should be taken to
preserve letters or documents which might have legal importance, for example, adoption papers, releases, etc. Whenever
material of assorted sizes or weights is involved it is always wise
to consider whether the item may be copied into the text without loss of value.

## Procedures and Mechanics

Workers have always debated the question as to how much of
mechanics or procedure belongs in records. Clearly it is a waste

[6]For the contents and style of letters, see Chapter 9.

of time to write "Telephoned Grand Central Station and ascertained that train left at 3:15; called at home; waited while mother dressed Johnny, and took him in a bus to the station." If during these arrangements either Johnny's or his mother's behavior or conversation was significant, a descriptive entry might be valuable, but the worker's behavior and technique were in this example unimportant. Pioneer social case workers, trying to learn a technique of social investigation in the face of much hostile criticism, did describe routine operations with more detail than would be useful today, when such procedures are quite well understood, accepted, and obvious. For a teaching record a surgeon may describe an operation carefully, but he does not begin the record with his washing up with green soap. In case work, as we have said before, the student must be taught not to neglect the obvious, but this does not mean that he should record details of the obvious. The search in all social case work is for the significant, and recording should be only of material which we think has (out of the world of things which one sees and touches in any social situation) at least potential significance for treatment. The careful writer tends thus to delete mechanical details and to give results alone, whenever the steps involved would be readily inferred by another professional worker. The best rule about recording procedures is to report only what is unusual or atypical. Thus, we would not say: "Called and found Mrs. Smith at home"; but we would say: "Called for the third consecutive day and was unable to find Mrs. Smith, although she has said that she had no work at all." Workers should distinguish the recording of "process"[7]—that is, the case work process itself—from those administrative secondary procedures which are part of office routine. The latter should be minimal in the case record.

Indexing,[8] or marginal notes, may be done formally or informally. Index headings may refer to the main movements in a case: application, eligibility study, social history, diagnostic statement, closing entry; or to contents: presenting problem, health, school, work history, finances, or the like; or to pro-

[7]See Chapter 4.
[8]For a good discussion of marginal indexing, see Bristol, *op. cit.*, p. 62, *et seq.*

cedure: letter sent, home visit; the last type being of the least value. Most indexing is so poorly done as to have little value, but if writers with a clear sense of significance should index the chief themes it would no doubt add to readability, especially in records following a largely chronological pattern. Sometimes marginal notes are all one sees of the worker's analytical thinking. While this is better than nothing, diagnosis and evaluation in the text should be encouraged[9] instead. The practice of letting diagnostic or evaluation summaries stand out through the use of a colored sheet has considerable merit.

## Style

Many writers of records are interested in such arrangements of detail as commonly are thought to make up style. A professional style is as elusive in case records as is style in a sonnet or letter or a novel, because "style" is a shorthand word for expressing a complex of behavior, emotion, and thought. Good usage, good grammar, good construction of sentences and paragraphs are the basis of all style. Each case is a sort of abstraction, a professionally conceived body of elements relevant to our purposes, which does make for some unity. The meaning of a case professionally emerges as the case progresses, so that our grasp of significance is dynamic rather than ultimate, practical rather than theoretical. A good professional style means that back of it is a good diagnostician or there will be no problem-solving unity. Back of a good professional style is mastery of the treatment process with clarity of direction because one knows what we and the client are doing together.

The device of parentheses used sometimes for the worker's questions and comments becomes tiring to the eye if it is repeated constantly through successive pages. When large blocks of interview material are given, no devices seem to make an easily read page. The completely unbroken paragraph presents about as many difficulties as the use of italics and parentheses. Beginning each speaker's remark on a fresh line makes reading easier but is wasteful of space. Although paragraphing must often be arbitrary, some breakup of a too close-packed effect

[9]See Chapters 6 and 7.

should be attempted. The best solution is that of selectivity in the choice of interviews to be fully or in part reproduced. With extensive use of "process"[10] reproduction, the awkwardness of which is undeniable for general use, marginal indexing, parentheses, italics, indentation, and frequent breaking up of the solid page afford, if not over-elaborated, some relief to the eye, but it is better to use process sparingly, and reduce the quantity in favor of significance.

· SUMMARY

The record is for use, which means that within an orderly, well-organized framework workers must be able to find the significant facts easily. One need not be "literary" to write a clear, brief, accurate, objective, usable record, but one must be a professionally disciplined person to do so. Format, structure, arrangement and style should all be conducive to readability. The trend is toward a unified record rather than a record assembled by departments. Supplementary records by technicians or consultants should be kept at a minimum. All important contacts with the client and his family should be reported in the unit record. Workers should train themselves to use the record, not depend upon the notebook to refresh the memory. A good rule is: never leave in the head what should be jotted down in the notebook, and never leave in the notebook what should be transcribed into the record. Likewise, a good rule for consultants and technicians is: anything which cannot be thrown away or posted to a card file, should be sent to the unit record. Mechanics of office administration should be eliminated as far as possible. A good recording style is plain, clear, and as brief as the treatment use will permit. Accurate reporting rests on accurate observation and interviewing, but the habit of careful rather than careless statement is of great importance. Clarity and brevity are, at their best, attributes of analytical habit. To be brief because we have been unobservant or because little happened is no virtue, but to be brief because we really understand what we have seen or heard and so are able to give the essence of the matter, means nothing less than professional competence.

[10]See Chapter 4.

# 3

## THE RECORDING STYLE SHOULD SUIT THE CASE MATERIAL

THERE IS NO SUCH THING AS A MODEL RECORD, OR IF there were one's first duty would be to destroy it because people and situations and agencies differ each from the other, and the record should reflect these variations and particulars. A record should be a flexible instrument, responsive to the kind of case, to agency function, to realistic conditions of practice, to what groups use the record, and to what clerical help is available. Good recording is based on good factual reporting and good thinking. These in turn are expressed through several basic methods: narrative, the story form of writing; summary for condensation and recapitulation; and interpretation to show the worker's reflection about the case materials.[1] Any record should show clearly the nature of the problem presented or the request made; what the client thinks and feels about his situation and the experience of getting help; what the worker thinks about the situation; what worker and client do about it; what relevant family, group, and community factors are involved; what the change or movement and outcome are.

Good style and good contents are inseparable. Good style is also responsive to agency purposes. A style weighted with terms used in "therapy" would not be suitable for a public assistance record. Good style finally is always the product of good thinking, which should result in direct, clear, plain writing. To paraphrase a few points from an excellent handbook,[2] one may say that the principles of good recording are:

[1]The several basic styles in recording are each fully discussed in succeeding chapters.
[2]Robert Graves, and Alan Hodge, *Reader over Your Shoulder; a Handbook for Writers of English Prose*, Chapter X, p. 127.

It should always be made clear who are involved in the situation; who is addressing whom on what subject, and what are the sources of information;

The details of every significant subject or situation should be given and there should never be any doubt where something happened or is expected to happen;

There should never be any doubt as to when, how much or how many;

and the writer would add:

One should not record the self-evident, the insignificant, the familiar and the repetitive.

A good rule for content and style should be: look at this applicant; talk to him; write about him, his attitudes, his needs, his relationships to others and to you. Don't ever see him, think about him or write about him as a *type*.

### · THE REPORTING OF FACTS

#### Narrative Style

The oldest form of case record available may be compared to a diary; an account of the steps taken by the case worker. However, even in these early case records, one comes across an occasional summary of events over a long period of time. The content was always that of objective facts and happenings since the worker's impressions, especially when conveyed through the lavish use of adjectives, were discouraged. Workers had not yet learned how and for what purposes to observe behavior, and diagnosis was still undeveloped. Mary Richmond, a great reader of case records, always used to say that she preferred the "open structure," that is, diary type, of record because she could see everything for herself.

Entries of this type have changed little over the past thirty years, and indeed they are probably still the most common. Compare, for instance, the following similar pairs of entries more than twenty years apart:

*Dec. 19, '08.*—Visited school and saw teacher and principal Acton. . . . Mrs. Babbit said at first B. was very troublesome, would pout and sulk and sometimes scream at top of lungs when crossed in any way or when corrected; but that by talking kindly to her and insisting on obedience she had improved very much.[3]

*Nov. 3, '33.*—The teacher stated to the worker that the girl's difficulty is stealing which she began before her mother's death. She steals only from her own home such things as her father's shirts, cans of fruit, dishes and table linen. She gets on well at school and seems to be no problem there. (From a visiting teacher record.)

. . . . .

*Oct. 29, '07.*—Mrs. Dutton called at the office, makes very favorable report of B. Says she is capable and willing, is saving her money and spends it in a sensible way; the other day bought pair of rubbers for self. . . . Mrs. Dutton feels she understands B. and says she needs affection.[4]

*Sept. 2, '31.*—Mr. Smith called at the office to make final arrangements for camp for Willie. He made the necessary deposit of $5 and got from us list of clothing. He showed interest and concern that everything should be properly attended to. He asked worker to come and see his wife as soon as possible to tell her about the sewing class as he thinks she needs an interest since her mother's death. (From a child placing record.)

Although the decade 1920–1930 saw a rapid development in the use of the partially or wholly summarized record,[5] some agencies have never departed far from narrative style recording, permitting themselves at the most a "diagnostic" summary; and even when monthly summaries are used, these appear in condensed narrative rather than topical arrangements. Narrative is always thought of as the descriptive style. When the process of the interview or of group interaction is being described, this is known in professional terminology as "process" recording.

## Summarized Style

If the careful reporting of events and behavior in narrative style is important in developing the hearing ear and the seeing eye, one may add that selecting and organizing material helps the mind to think. Summaries not only point up but they point

[3]The above illustration is taken from printed but unpublished case records of the years noted. *Charity Organization Society Bulletin*, Vol. III, Mary E. Richmond, ed. Russell Sage Foundation, 1911 and 1912.
[4]*Ibid.*
[5]Judge Baker Foundation, Case Studies No. 1, 1922–23.

in to the meaning and relative importance of the material gathered. A careful summary made at appropriate intervals reduces bulk, clarifies direction, and saves the worker's time. The summary [6] is commonly assumed to be a review or recapitulation of material which has already appeared in the record. In the judgment of the writer, we should also include under summary, entries compiled from case notes *not* previously recorded. This disagrees with some, though not all, of the authorities. Summaries may be either topically arranged or may appear as condensed chronological narrative. Social study summaries are usually of the former type; periodic or treatment summaries, of the latter. The reason for this is that the objective facts of the life history are easily grouped, whereas the treatment process is at once more fluid and more unified.

The social study or social history (anamnesis, as the hospital calls it) is often blocked under topics. One should understand that events which take place before the case is opened must be distinguished from events modified by the agency—or persons and events affected by our treatment. Antecedent history of objective data, taken in a matter-of-fact, question-and-answer way, by the case worker, is usually condensed into a topical summary. Such factual summaries may be arranged by *subjects*—for example, eligibility data, background, health, parents, school, work history, etc.—or by *persons*—Mr. Smith, Mrs. Smith, Tommy—or by a combination. Most agencies use a summary outline which, following the main currents of life experience,

[6] Mrs. Bristol, in her *Handbook on Social Case Recording*, p. 119, restricted the word to this usage: "The term *summary* is reserved by the present writer for use in connection with the process of bringing together, reviewing, or 'summarizing' material which has *previously* appeared in the record in one form or another. It is true that most summaries are arranged in topical form, but the fact which serves to distinguish them from what is here designated as *topical recording* is that they contain no 'original' material, that is, material recorded for the first time." Mrs. Sheffield, in *Social Case History*, earlier used the word in the same way to mean "a brief account containing the sum or substance of an earlier account." Dr. Southard, in *The Kingdom of Evils*, p. 537, says: "In the discussions of social workers there seems to be an uncertainty of opinion as to the nature and uses of a summary. Some look to it for a full presentation of the case, a complete digest of the history, which is recorded elsewhere in the form of interviews and letters. We conceive the summary as the briefest possible statement of the essential facts of the case, following in the form the outline used for collecting the data. The judgment of the worker in selecting the essential facts necessarily enters into the summary."

emphasizes topics of especial interest to its own purposes. Some workers imagine because history is taken in a certain way that it must be recorded in the same way. This is not true. Skill in interviewing determines how history is obtained. Subsequently it should be written up in the way best suited to the material. Treatment summaries, as indicated above, are usually shown in condensed narrative style, sometimes with process effects if interviewing has been the chief medium of treatment. Such summaries may be condensation of a month or three months, or any suitable period. Single entries written in condensed narrative, as opposed to process style, are not called summaries. These are, perhaps, the most common type of entry and fall under the ordinary classification of "narrative" chronological writing.

Some argue that chronological, as-it-happened recording, always shows case work method far better than summary, and that summaries make for rigidity. The proponents of summary argue that summarizing itself is a discipline in analysis; that day-by-day recording burdens the record with unselected material, much of it of doubtful value; that the practice of holding dictation until a sense of unity and direction can be elicited from the stream of treatment makes for better contents. Whenever summary is used, however, sources of material must always be clearly indicated; and if dictation is delayed for any length of time rough notes must be kept so that nothing important will be overlooked during the absence of the worker or in case of a change of workers. Balance should be retained between material which lends itself readily to summary and that which does not. A long chronological record becomes unreadable unless supported by summaries at suitable places.

· THE MEANING OF FACTS

## Interpretive Style, Diagnosis and Evaluation

The significance of a record lies in the meaning of the case to us as practitioners. In a literal sense we have to stop to think. It is not enough to observe closely and report accurately, nor is it enough to think silently or even aloud or in conference. Our obligation is to write down what is the matter, that is, what is the problem, how the client is getting along, and what he is doing about his situation, what is the nature of our service or help or treatment. A record is not a professional document, nor is it entirely a reliable document, if there is no social interpretation therein. But, says the worker, "Is it not better to let the facts speak for themselves?" It is good to have facts, and plenty of them, in the record, but it is better to have also the opinion of the worker who at first hand is reporting the facts. A trained eye will derive truer significance from social data than an untrained eye, but an eye trained to see, hear, and report accurately, serving a mind trained to reflect, is best of all.

But does not a recorded interpretation condition both the worker himself and subsequent readers? Yes, to some extent, but not necessarily permanently or rigidly or wrongfully. The point is that since the worker is using a hypothesis he had better state it fearlessly and test it, and let others test it. The remedy for poor interpretation is more, not less, practice at it. There are two important complementary ways in which one reacts to facts—diagnosis and evaluation.

We must always try to understand the nature of the problem ("diagnosis") we are asked to treat, and because we work toward social ends, social values are inextricably present ("evaluation"). The toughest sort of intellectual effort is involved in trying to wrest out the meaning of the case, particularly since diagnostic terminology and a conceptual scheme of values has not been systematically worked out for social case work, and the chief importance of professional education lies precisely in its intellectual disciplines which deepen knowledge, clarify goals, and tend to greater development and control of skill. The record is a medium of communication, and diagnostic precision represents the highest level of communication we can achieve therein.

## · PERSON, TENSE, TERMINOLOGY

Questions concretely raised about style have to do with tense, person, phrasing, use of slang, professional terminology, beheaded sentences (subject omitted), elliptical sentences, and so on. Tense should, of course, follow ordinary grammatical rules,

the point being raised because of the practice of putting interviews in the present tense, for example, "worker asks (asked)
Mrs. Smith if she would like to go to the country"; "worker
visits (visited) the Jenkins family, finds (found) Jimmy at home
alone"; "Mr. Brown replies (replied) that he was deeply upset."
Some recorders select the present tense because it seems a more
vivid or dramatic tense. But this practice is difficult to sustain
for routine events, and writers often slip back into the past tense
without noticing the shift. Stenographers, unless trained to use
the present tense, easily revert to the past. While there is no
special reason against the use of the present tense, especially in
fully reproduced interviews, the past remains the more accepted.
Irregular forms of sentences omitting subject or verb do not
materially shorten the record, and offer no special advantages.
Good sentence structure with selection and condensation is
always preferable to mannerisms and idiosyncrasies.

At one time on the face sheet and in the text persons were referred to as 1–2–3–4–5, "one" being the man, "two" the woman,
and the children being numbered thereafter. Later this style
yielded to "man," "woman," "child," and now the accepted
usage is "Mr. Brown," "Mrs. Brown," and "Tommy"; with,
however, the usual alternatives of "mother," "father," "foster
mother," "sister," as called for.

The use of the third person is the most common and probably
the most appropriate for agencies in which the use of social resources and the manipulation of environmental factors are dominant services. This is much to be preferred to the first person
plural or "editorial we" ("we said," "we suggested," "it occurred to us," "we wondered if," even, with a touch of absurdity,
"we smiled as we sat down"). The "editorial we" is the correct
person for interagency letters, but not for clients, when the first
person singular should be used. The first person singular is
suitable in recording interviews in which the case work relationship is the chief medium of treatment (therapy). It is not the
experience of the writer that when the student discovers the
"professional self" he begins to use "I." Rather is it true that
all untrained and young workers spontaneously use "I." It will

be found that the first person singular used by inexperienced workers gives a peculiarly naïve quality to the recording. Probably only staffs of well-trained workers should use this person routinely and then only with highly articulated interviewing skill. It may be suggested that "I" is a simple, natural usage for diagnostic comment, even when the third person is otherwise used; for example, "Murray said, 'You don't know the half of it!' When worker said, 'Tell me the other half,' Murray began a scared recital of a stealing episode. *I could see the boy was beginning to lay aside his defenses.*" "I think that" is simpler than "it was worker's impression that."

The words and phrases used in records, more than the person, determine whether the style is formal or informal, dignified or decorated. A simple, direct, lucid style is always to be preferred. Probation and court records have shown a tendency to legal phraseology and sometimes to overelaborate diction. The present trend in court records is away from legalistic terminology to plain English, and with all records the swing is away from psychiatric word borrowings. "Foreign" words or phrases borrowed from psychiatry and medicine may be employed only if they have been thoroughly naturalized in social work: "She herself has a somewhat rigid attitude, answers questions with simply 'yes' or 'no,' does not talk spontaneously, has a frank, expressionless *facies*, and talks in a monotonous way." The word *facies* here is to be questioned, as would be "libidinal security," "cathexis," "oral character," if other words could be substituted without loss of sense. That the foreign, or imported, word is all too frequently overworked does not add to its charm. Ugly formations of words like "referrals" or "to contact" are in such common use that they may be good usage soon. In letters between social agencies we should be careful to use technical words and phrases only if they have wide and common professional acceptance, and in letters to laymen we should not use professional terms at all.

Social case work, like many other specialties, has developed a considerable vocabulary of technical words and phrases which become a sort of jargon quite incomprehensible and irritating to the uninitiated. Case workers should be cautioned to use the professional vocabulary critically, economically, and precisely in the record, and as little as possible on any other occasion.

The style of all case work recording is affected by the tendency toward considerable verbatim quotation, especially of what the client said. Conventional remarks and realistic practical discussion are rarely given, but workers skilled in recognizing and responding to feeling as expressed in language pick up and repeat words and imagery used by the client, to clarify conflicts, bring emotional material nearer to consciousness, and so on. Only workers competent in the more therapeutic aspects of case work are, perhaps, able to do this successfully, but if such material is used with discrimination and insight it may be appropriately brought into the record. Such workers keep full notes in their notebooks, from which selected interviewing passages may be dictated in a way to show both the process and direction of the interview.

There is very little to say about slang except to repeat the caution of those most persuasive grammarians, the brothers Fowler,[7] that slang is meant to be spoken, not written. The practice of quoting interviews verbatim has brought this problem acutely to the front. Here good taste and a sense of what is significant must be the control. It is hard to know when the slang is deliberately chosen as the best means of revealing a client's attitude or when the writer is tempted by the vigorous and picturesque. If the reader's attention is directed to the style rather than to the content in a professional record, it is an indication of weakness.

Although we need not be inhibited from giving precise material which, whether pleasant or unpleasant, reveals important motivation, it is the young worker usually who repeats unnecessary intimacies, particularly those of a sex nature, which, in direct quotation, often are vulgarisms. We have accustomed ourselves[8] to this in interviews on sex behavior when the person's

[7] H. W. and F. T. Fowler, *The King's English.*
[8] Susan Isaacs, *Social Development in Young Children.* This gives the behavior and conversations of children in a way and for a purpose that cannot be offensive to the serious reader, and child guidance records habitually record such material so plainly and simply that it is unobtrusive.

own choice of word and concept may be significant, but we
should take care that our selection is appropriate to the uses of
the record.

Like slang, criticism of cooperating agencies and persons is
better not written, and if it must be written should be as factual
and objective as possible. One is safer with careful description
here than with adjectives and adverbs. Agency relations outlast
most workers' individual contacts with them, and current impressions may serve only to caricature some incident. When
significant client attitudes are expressed in criticism of an agency,
these projections belong in the record.

The objection to such a comment as the one quoted below is
that, although it may quite well be true, it leaves in the memory
a distasteful impression which cannot be erased even after workers and program have been changed. Because it was not handled
by the worker in the interview, the passage here has merely the
effect of gossip.

Mrs. P. said that she had gone to the Church Institute, where they
told her that they couldn't help her. She said that the man there had
told her, "A lot of nerve coming to us! Let the Home Relief Bureau
give you what you need!"

If the criticism is flavored with patronage or sarcasm, the
comment is no more endearing:

Miss Small impressed the probation officer on first meeting as being a
frustrated and neurotic individual. Apparently from her mispronuncia-
tion of the terms commonly used by a psychiatrist or a more modern
educator, one would think that this was the first psychiatric report
she had seen. The probation officer made no headway whatever. Upon
leaving she thanked Miss Small for revealing so plainly the cause of
Angelo's misconduct.

Such terms as "grateful," "antagonistic," "uncooperative,"
and so forth, suggest an enquiry into the worker's attitudes as
well as recording. Here again the use of quotations or a description of behavior is more effective than phrases which are, in
effect, a "label."

One of the most confusing questions for a young worker is
whether or not to put into the record those things which the

client tells him "personally." This problem is involved in the worker's relationship with the client, as well as in the matter of recording. One wonders whether the information which the worker hesitates to record should have been secured from the client. The worker may think that achieving personal liking from the client is an end in itself, rather than that the client-worker relationship is a means to the end of working with the individual through sympathy and understanding. Some workers feel it "good work" if they can lead the client on to speak of highly confidential and personal affairs, and they may be helped to see that they are listening to the client's story only because they represent the agency. It is necessary to know why the client gave the worker the "confidential" material. Was it because the worker "led him on" because it flattered him to receive such confidences; was it the client's great need to talk about the situation; or was it an effort on the part of the client to gain "sympathy" and perhaps divert the worker from other areas? These things affect the problem of gauging just what material is confidential. The same type of information which may be "confidential" to one individual is repeatedly discussed by another individual without conflict. When records are likely to be available to a number of non-professional people, it is necessary to use restraint both in content and style. Workers should distinguish between material which, though unpleasant or painful, is relevant to the problem and material which is irrelevant. The former belongs in the record; the latter probably not.

### · SUMMARY

There is no such thing as a model or pattern record, and in the professional record skill in practice and skill in recording are so closely interdependent as to be almost indistinguishable. Style will be conditioned throughout by the case work concepts and practices reported. The best records contain not only objective facts, events, and behavior, but are purposed to bring out clearly diagnostic thinking and treatment as well. Narrative and summarized writing are equally useful, and a well-balanced record will employ both styles. In a professional record interpretation of the meaning of the case is as essential as the reporting of facts.

Records may be short or long, but their constant use—beyond the value of the content itself—makes readability the most important single factor. The interest value or readability of a professional record derives directly and solely from the nature of the problems and the treatment, not from picturesqueness or drama. The style, then, that brings out significant elements in the case work process most economically, accurately, and lucidly, is inevitably good style. Records used for teaching and study purposes will tend to include more details than do records used chiefly for practice. The ordinary rules of good English apply to making records readable, although symbols, abbreviations, and technical terms are permissible when the procedures indicated are in familiar professional use. Restraint and selection are always important, not only for the immediate purpose of brevity, but for the reason that in many agencies access to records is not sufficiently guarded. Workers should use a professional vocabulary with precision and restraint in the record, and as little as possible with the larger community. The client's own words to a trained ear have significance as clues to feeling and, therefore, may be selectively reproduced in the record.

# 4

# NARRATIVE IS A GOOD STYLE FOR REPORTING FACTS

As WE INDICATED IN THE LAST CHAPTER, NARRATIVE is the primary style for the social case record. It is the oldest story form and the most familiar. It is the style found in newspapers and magazines. It is the way we speak of the days' events: it is the way we write letters; it is the way we keep diaries. Students use it naturally and are encouraged through it to learn how to observe and how to listen. Good case work operates on a factual basis, and a good case record contains a sufficiency of pertinent fact. Facts include not only objective social and cultural and economic events, the happenings and circumstances in the case, but also behavior, whether gesture, movement, or the behavior of a child in a play situation, or verbal behavior as in the interview situation. It is no accident that we lean heavily on narrative, or "running" style for the fluidity of interpersonal relations. The thoughts and feelings of the client expressed in what he says and does are of great significance, and while condensation of the more objective data in the record is often desirable, psychological "evidence," which calls for a delicate, well-attuned eye and ear, may be demonstrated through a style which better shows the associative relationship of ideas, stimulus and response. Single interviews or series of interviews on a relationship basis are hard to reproduce through any medium, but since it is extremely difficult to indicate feeling except through conversation and behavior, most workers attempt a narrative reproduction rather than summary—another possibility being a highly diagnostic method of writing, discussed in a later chapter.[1]

[1]See Chapter 6.

The earliest reporting was largely that of episodes, events—the more obvious material and social facts. "Behavior" was ignored; "conduct" was recorded usually in a judgmental way. Clinical observation and reporting of behavior were scarcely possible until psychiatric contents became assimilated in case work practice. Until the motivation of behavior is understood, case work relationship cannot be accurately described, which is only to re-emphasize that until the case worker knows how to see significant things he cannot record with dependable accuracy. His perceptions in the field of personality will depend on his apperceptions, based on his real equipment and training. Learning to recognize the defenses such as rationalization, denial, displacement, and so forth, is like learning to use a microscope intelligently. There is constant interaction between what one understands and what one is able to see. Noting affective quality, the emotional overtones in an interview, always requires trained observation and listening.

In the first two decades of the century when workers had concerned themselves objectively with the study and analysis of facts and events, records were episodic and static like photographs. In the third decade, under psychiatric and especially psychoanalytical influence, behavior came to be studied, first descriptively, and then more and more for its meaning to the client. As the assumption was made that only the client could give the meaning for him of his problem, interest turned from patterns of history to immediate conversational behavior, or the interview. The attempt "to see things in their own order and conviction," as Spinoza phrased it, was precipitated into case work.[2] The first stage, in which workers turned away from a directed interview under the mistaken impression that to abandon dictating to the client meant abandoning control of the process, was known as "passivity." Interviews lasted for hours; records meandered on for pages; everything the client said was recorded. Interviews were full of pauses which the case worker,

[2]Virginia Robinson, in *A Changing Psychology in Social Case Work*, p. 143, says, "History will take its place in the relationship . . . as one of the client's reactions. It will come into the record at whatever time and place the client needs to make use of it. . ."

on theory, did not break. Records actually recorded these pauses, which were thought to show (as they sometimes do, of course) pain spots and resistances. The client's verbalization was fully recorded; the worker, little more than a participant observer, ventured only such remarks as "You must be worried about that," or "It must be hard for you," or "wondered" some gentle stimulus to set the client off again—so the process itself was a one-sided affair.

Fortunately for both the client and the record, a growing understanding of ego psychology has brought the field back to external reality and to more active roles in helping. The record remains "client centered," but the interview process is two-sided, with the worker's role again articulated. Putting it succinctly, one might say that the first stage showed what the worker told the client; the second stage what the client told the worker; the third or current stage shows a developed process of interaction. Today, events and objective social data are usually reported in *condensed*, important observations of behavior or emotionally charged interviews, in *extended* or "process" style. Process is to condensed narrative what slow motion is to the ordinary picture. On the film one may see every detail of the hurdler's motion in clearing the bar, or of the tennis star performing a volley. So in the verbatim recording of the interview, or the play interview, or the group interaction, one may see the details of technique. While only the dictaphone gives scientifically precise reproduction, a trained ear, eye and memory, supported by notes, can be depended on for reasonable accuracy. What was inaccurate in a single interview can usually be corrected through a sequence of interviews since, as we know, people tend to bring up again and again the things which trouble them.

## Narrative, Condensed Style

This is a generally useful form for all types of case work agencies. It is almost always to be preferred for reporting acts of practical helpfulness, events, and most collateral visits or conferences. It may be used for the contents of the interview in all instances except when the process itself and the use of relationship have special significance. The following excerpt shows condensed narrative style with one bit of process effectively used in the second paragraph to underline the emotion. If the worker had responded more directly to the emotion—"So you see. . .," it would have been a better interview and the process effect perhaps would be more justified in the record.

Mr. L. lost his job in September, 1939, and following that had received 12 weeks of Unemployment Insurance Benefits at $15.00 a week. He produced a statement from the Universal Iron Works, To Whom It May Concern, saying that Mr. L. had been employed by the firm from 1930 until Sept. 7, 1939, and had lost the job when the company went out of business following the death of the owner. The letter stated that Mr. L. was a conscientious and competent worker, and was highly recommended for employment as an iron worker's helper. He also showed a statement indicating that he had received UIB for 13 weeks, and that he had exhausted the possibility of benefits. He had brought both these statements because he thought they might be requested by the worker. He was not a member of a union, but had gone to all of the iron work concerns that he could locate and had filed an application for a job in all of them. He mentioned some of these specifically by name and address. He had several friends who had also been employed at the Universal Iron Works, who had been successful in getting jobs and they had recommended him in several places. He was in hopes that he would eventually be placed with the Atlas Iron Works or the American Construction Company.

Mr. L. paused here and said to the worker, "So you see, there is not much else for me to do, but apply for help." Interviewer asked how they had been managing to meet their expenses since he lost his employment, and he said that following the loss of his job in September they had used the $70 which his wife had saved at home, plus his last week's pay to pay their September rent; to buy heavy clothing for the children, and to pay their household expenses until he received his UIB. After that they had managed on the $15 a week which he got from UIB, and with some help from his family and his wife's they had been able to manage part of their expenses, but he owed $57 to the landlord and over $6 to the gas and electric company, and also he was behind on his payments on a $40 bill owed to the Flatbush Furniture Company. Mr. L. had not actually stopped paying any of these, but he had not been able to pay the whole amount necessary so that he was behind with all of these bills.

There is rarely any good reason for verbatim reporting of interviews other than those of the intimate "patient group." In application interviews or with sustained relationship, it is important often to give the person's own words and to show the verbal role of the case worker, but in a collateral[3] visit typically one is conferring rather than interviewing. Emotional expressions are beyond recapture by the end of the session; one has been, for better or worse, sensitive or insensitive, skillful or tactless, and there is no use pulling a long face over it afterward and taking a page to reproduce everyone's attitudes. It is simpler to give the gist of the discussion, with or without comment, on the emotional overtones known best to the participant and observer at the time.

A school visit made on behalf of Alan, age 10, who was being tutored for reading, is in the usual condensed narrative style for "collateral" entries:

*6–13–44.* Visited school. Miss S. reported that Alan has made a remarkable improvement in his reading during the 5 months of tutoring. He now can read a strange book of about third-grade level. When she started with him he could not read at all. He has demanded a great deal of individual attention, but is responsive to her teaching. She feels that the best method to use with him is not to push him, but to encourage him to set his own pace. While I was there, she called Alan in and had him read at random from a strange third-grade reader, so that I could see his progress, and he could get the sense of satisfaction in showing me what he had accomplished. Alan read rather well, and although he was shy in manner, he seemed to enjoy showing me.

Alan is slow in drawing and is poorly coordinated in all manual studies. He still day-dreams, is inattentive to the teacher's directions, and the school questions if his I.Q. (126) is as high as he tested. His teacher doesn't want to promote him, but Miss S. is recommending promotion as she feels he will learn better if he goes along with his own class group. Miss S. expressed her concern about how Alan's mother plays into his sense of inferiority. For instance, the mother sends Alan

[3] A collateral in social case work is a contact made with someone other than a member of the immediate family

to school with clothes that are too small for him; she refused to allow him to participate in a school pageant because she did not want to provide the costume (which was simple). Finally, the teacher worked it out, and Alan was in the pageant and got a lot of fun out of it. I discussed the mother's personality and how we felt that at this point she was not able to understand Alan too well and, therefore, how important was the response she had been able to secure from the child.

If comment is given on a conference with a cooperating agency any hint of personal criticism, sarcasm, and condescension, should be avoided, the plain and reticent style being, as usual, in the best taste. A conference in which important contents emerged or decisions were arrived at might require full recording, but still the straight narrative or summarized style is the practical one for most occasions.

## Narrative, Process Style

Narrative may be elaborated to show interpersonal relations. We do not use process to recount events, anecdotes, episodes, trivial conversation, or procedures. Process is used to show the process or interaction within the interview or the play "interview" with a child, or to show group interaction.[4] It is not easy to reproduce feeling. The client may or may not express his feelings spontaneously through free association; only the skilled interviewer with any certainty may catch the overtones and react to them. As workers become secure in affective material and relationships they are more able to bring the emotion to the surface through responsive questioning, comment, restating conflict, and the like—"I can see you feel two ways about this." "It is quite natural that you both want to be with your little boy and feel you should work," or to a child client who, offering to water a window box for the worker, says anxiously, "I must be careful not to water your flowers too much." "What do you think would happen?" "They might die." "Do you think I would be mad at you?"

Process is a good medium when attention should be directed to attitudes, behavior, and motivation. It is often used for in-

[4]See S. R. Slavson, *An Introduction to Group Therapy*, for such material.

take or early interviews, when the client's feelings toward his situation and toward what he wants of the agency are likely to be particularly apparent. Part of an interview, "functional"[5] approach, will show this:

Mrs. E. apologizes profusely for coming three-quarters of an hour late for her appointment. Her eyes are red and swollen, and she is crying convulsively by the time we are seated. I acknowledge how real this trouble is for her and that she certainly has a right to refuse to accept the role of a part-time wife. But why is she telling me all this? Mrs. E. finally calms down a bit, saying that last time her main concern was help in deciding what to do about Alan. That is still on her mind, but now she also needs help for herself. She continues with a furious blast against the other woman; that she is going to "break her head with a stick." It is all her fault. She is leading Mr. E. astray, and telling him to stay with his family at the same time tying him to her. If only "someone" could explain this to Mr. E. and urge him to mend his ways, perhaps that would work. I wonder if by "someone" she means the agency. She admits this. I tell Mrs. E. that we have no right to intercede with Mr. E. on her behalf, but my saying so does not answer the problem for her. We talk for a while about how futile all of her efforts up to this point have been in getting outside people to patch things up between them.

Mrs. E. refers to my comment that her feelings in this count, carrying it a bit further to initiate discussion about legal separation. In considering this as a possibility, Mrs. E. immediately raises her fear that a support order might be for less than what she is getting from Mr. E. now. If that were so she will have to go to work. How will she ever get a job and take care of the house? I say that many of these fears are justified, but that only she can decide whether it is worth making the break with all the uncertainties involved, or go on trying to keep things as they are. If Mr. E. doesn't want to be related to his family and her in a more positive way we cannot provide the force to bring about such a change. Part of this belongs to Mrs. E., the decision to set up a home separately. Of course no one could expect that such a drastic change could be sustained single handed, and we may be able to help her follow through on such a plan for change. But something would have to be settled between her and Mr. E. and within her own mind

[5]Agency structure and function being accorded special significance in the helping process.

first. If this is what she wants our help with, we will have to consult with Mr. E. about the break-up of his home.

Mrs. E. then asks about the court and what that would involve. She is calmer now, and as we discuss this she seems to take it in as a possibility, as though groping for a way to get her feelings into action. Only at this point is she able to bring in the fact that she has already consulted a lawyer who suggested some kind of legal separation. Her chance of getting more adequate support seemed better this way. I comment that actually she has already taken one step toward finding out whether she really wants separate maintenance. . . . I let Mrs. E. know that for us to go on here will mean her having to consult further with the lawyer, and that way she will perhaps know a little better in view of what she could get out of separation, if she wants to go through with it or not.

Two examples showing conscious use of relationship in modified process follow:

Mrs. Hand said she had not heard from us in so long, she was afraid we'd forgotten her. I explained that a change in workers often involves a lapse of time and recognized that in her case it had probably been difficult for her since she'd had such a close relationship with Miss Brown. I asked her what made her feel we'd forgotten her; did she perhaps almost hope we had? Mrs. Hand smiled and said she felt she had gained a great deal from her contact with Miss Brown, but she wasn't sure about coming to see a new worker. I encouraged her to speak of her contact with Miss Brown, which she did at great length, showing much positive feeling and a strong sense of dependence. With some encouragement Mrs. Hand was able to verbalize some of her negative feeling toward having a new worker, and I gave her much acceptance in this area. As she became more at ease with me, she described how she'd changed in the past six months, i.e., in her relations with Willie, etc. She said she feels as if she has developed a "new self," and while Miss Brown was around she felt sure of this "new self." However, during the period when she had no worker at all, and even now that she has a new worker, she is rather mixed up about herself. I said it was natural that she should feel this way. I said Miss Brown had told me about their contact, and I gave Mrs. Hand a good deal of praise about her improved ability to handle whatever difficulties Willie was presenting. Mrs. Hand again spoke of her successful contact with Miss Brown and the fears that she will revert back to her "old self." I said it sounded as though Mrs. Hand was afraid of this "old self." I wondered what it was she feared. Perhaps I could help her to become more sure of her "new self." Mrs. Hand was silent for several minutes, then she said it had been some time before she was able to share as much as she had with Miss Brown. Perhaps since she remembers that at her first interview with Miss Brown she felt somewhat the same about her as she does about me now, she and I will become just as close. . . . Mrs. Hand said she feels things are better between her and Mr. Hand also; he is beginning to take notice of her ability to manage things in his absence, and when he left after his furlough complimented her on how much better he had found Willie. I remarked that she'd done these things on her own since she was not seeing Miss Brown at the time. She responded to this by enthusiastically relating another incident.

· · · · ·

Mrs. J. was in a decidedly hostile and defensive mood in reaction to her interview. She told me the recommendations given to her by the doctor and was quite annoyed by the whole thing. She said that the doctor had told her not to do anything for one or two years about placing the boy or further hospitalizing him. She wondered what the doctor expected her to do in the meantime, go crazy? Sam has continued to be extremely difficult, is nervous, cranky, screaming, biting, won't sit down to eat. She has trouble with him over everything. Mrs. J. talks with him, yells at him, punishes him. She cannot stand the constant death threats against herself and hits him for this. She still has to lie down with him if she wants him to go to sleep or to rest for a while during the day. Sam is fearful of the dark and will not go into a room alone unless the light is on. It's all right if his brother is in the room. He tells his mother that she is worse than a stepmother. On the street it is impossible for her to be near Sam because he immediately starts to curse her and use dirty words. Mrs. J. was disgusted and asked Sam what he thought he would do if she was no longer there—if she died. Sam said that his father would take care of him.

I gave Mrs. J. a great deal of sympathy today, particularly in view of the fact that she had to put up with this boy's very difficult behavior by herself without her husband's assistance. I also acknowledged with her during her complaints against the doctor that this only intensified her own feelings of having to bear the brunt of it herself. She revealed as she talked that while she had stopped taking as frequent temperatures as before, she would not feel comfortable within herself if she did not take it once a day or perhaps once in two or three days. At the same time she is concerned because he continues to run and become overheated. She complained bitterly that she was told by the doctor not to keep after the boy so much. She wondered if the doctor had a child, one that had been sick and almost died; how he thought a mother could stop watching over her own child. I commented that again she felt that she was being criticized and being told that she was bad for doing what she thought was right.

As the interview wore on she relaxed somewhat, felt a little reassured, able to talk somewhat more concretely about her handling of Sam during this difficult period. She told me that she was trying very hard not to threaten the boy, that she had always tried hard not to frighten him unnecessarily. I gather that she was much more conscious of what she was saying to him although as yet her procedure had not changed. I reviewed with her, therefore, the fact that to Sam, having been sent away from home for such a long period of time, any separation from home had come to mean being punished by his mother for his bad behavior. Mrs. J. became upset as she protested that she had only sent him away because of his health. I assured her that I knew that, and that almost everybody knew that what she had done had been for Sam's health, but that to the boy it had meant something else because he had been so difficult and so bad with her so often in the past. I indicated that Sam now has to be helped to see that being bad would not bring further placement; that his mother really wanted him home even though he was so difficult and even though he was so very trying to her. Even as I spoke with Mrs. J. I felt that she squared her shoulders as if for battle, and in a most heroic tone told me that she had gone through so much that she would be able to go through a little more.

From a child placing record—attitudes, behavior, and relationship being the focus of attention:

We were late for the doctor's appointment, and I took Hans downstairs to undress while I went for his medical record. When I explained I was going to get it, he said, "No, no, no!" his voice getting louder until he was almost shouting. Before I had a chance to say anything he added imperiously, "Hurry!" After his examination he wanted a great deal of help with dressing. I acceded to this since I felt he needed "babying.". . .

I had promised him a balloon, and on our way to the 5 and 10 he said he was going to have a party and invite me. He would give me "ice cream and jelly and a punch in the belly." I said he was quite angry with me today, but he brushed this aside and went into the store, pushing ahead through the crowds without turning or waiting for me. On the bus he immediately occupied the seat he found. (Usually he offers it to me.) He addressed me in a cold, commanding fashion. "Sit there!" "Fix my balloon!" I was not sitting near enough to help him with the balloon, which was stuck together, but said pleasantly I would help him with it when we got off the bus. He tried to fix it himself, became angry and frustrated, and almost wept. They had given him a no-good balloon and he was going to take it back. I said I was sorry we couldn't go back, but if it were no-good I could exchange it for him and send him a good one.

At lunch he was hostile. He looked very warm, but declined to remove his jacket and hood. He got up and bounced his balloon in the path of the waitress, and even took off my hat and dropped it behind a chair. . . .

Hans asked where we were going next. I said we would go to the Tiding Over Home. Hans said, "That's what I hate about this day." I said I thought that was why he had been so angry with me. Tears came to his eyes and he nodded his head. He asked how long he would stay there, and I said I thought it would be several weeks. Hans said, after that he would return to the foster home. I said I knew his foster mother loved him, but I did not think he could go back. He asked why. I said he knew foster mother was quite sick, and taking care of three children seemed just too much for her. If we were to go back after she got well it would be too much for her all over again. Hans did not comment. . . .

On the subway he cuddled against me and was almost "himself" again, but subdued. I told him we were looking for a good home where he would be able to stay for a long time. Hans hoped we would find a good place, not "a place where they beat children." I asked whether he had been in such a place. He said at the N.'s they punished you "if you even came in the house with dirt on your rubbers." Before that, his grandfather had a switch to hit him with. He told of these experiences as if he were making sensational disclosures. I said we would be very careful about the place we chose, and would make sure it was a place where the people would be good to him. When I attempted to discuss further the situation in the foster home, Hans said, "Please don't talk about that, it makes me feel like crying."

An excerpt from a family record shows a child acting out in play what goes on at home.

Gloria started to give a running commentary of the actions as she played with the doll figures. "The girl doll walks around the house, walks upstairs, thinks she is going to bed. Oh no, she looks at the mirror and out of the window and decides she won't go to bed after all." Describes in detail how a bed is made, where you put each cover, etc., tells us that the mother knows just how to do it even if the girl doesn't. "The girl walks downstairs, she knows nothing, she sits downstairs on a chair, she hears a rap at the door. Mother comes in and says to the girl, 'Go away.' " (Why does she say that.) "Oh, she is mad, she is tired and wants to go to bed." Gloria walks the mother upstairs and puts her into the larger bed. As soon as the mother is sleeping the girl tiptoes upstairs to see what the mother is doing. Gloria gets quite excited at this point, and asks whether she can look for another cover for the mother, covers up the mother some more, and announces that the mother is now snoring. Gloria has girl doll tiptoe upstairs to see the mother for a second and then fall down the stairs with a loud bang, as if she had done something forbidden. Mother wakes up on hearing this noise, yells at girl, tells her to "go out, will you?" in a very angry tone of voice. Mother adds that she has to work, that she is always glad to get rid of the baby. While mother is playing around with the radio the baby has either gone outside or has hidden some place. Mother now calls in a very sweet, artificial voice, "Darling, come in," and baby says "Yes, I will," knocks at the door. Mama announces sweetly that they are now going to have lunch.

Gloria then put the dish of beets on the dining room table. The girl announced that she doesn't like to eat it and the mother proceeds to "holler at her very loudly," and finally yells "Scram." The girl is so frightened that she falls out of the window with a loud bang. (Substitutes the baby doll.) Gloria seems a little frightened after she has dropped the baby, starts to crawl around on the floor to find her.

Suddenly with great exclamations of joy she finds the little figure that was used as the baby. Gloria remarks thoughtfully that perhaps it is a magic baby, it could fly and hide itself. (Do babies do that sort of thing?) "I don't know anything about babies." (Yes, I think you know a little.) "Oh, I only know about one baby." (Which one?) "Oh, that's my baby sister, it takes my toys all the time." (Do you get awfully mad at it?) "Not awfully mad, just a little bit mad."

The play interview, being a child's method of communication, is often given in process. As workers improve their skill in this field of observation they become able to discriminate and interpret as in other content and so to condense.

· *SUMMARY*

Narrative is the commonest style for reporting events, important interviews, and behavior. It runs from simple line-a-day type entries when case loads are heavy and objective data uppermost, to become a sophisticated medium for interpersonal relationships. Process style should be used only by skilled workers for important observations and interviews, not for procedural accounts or trivial conversations. When case workers say "record every detail lest some of it prove later to be significant," they are really admitting that they do not yet know how to recognize significant material, or they could select. In a young profession, as with a young worker, one may over-record because one does not know how to choose. As skill in interviewing grows, as workers are more able to precipitate movement in the interview itself, the contents become more vital and are more worth careful recording.

Application or early interviews are often given in the client's own words or in selective process; later interviews, only when the interplay is subtle or unusually significant. Ability to make diagnostic and evaluation comments may provide an effective short-cut instead of full-length verbatim. A whole series of treatment interviews,[6] may be just as effectively summarized as the facts of social study. Interviews in which the emotional values are minimal, or when the anger or aggression or fears are obvious, or in which the case work relationship is not involved to any great extent, or when social resources are realistically utilized by self-directing clients, or when information is sought on a straight question-answer basis, all this and much else can be condensed, arranged, and summarized, as we shall show hereafter.

In all case work interviews in which transference phenomena

[6]See pp. 53 and 57–60.

are prominent, because a treatment relationship is deeply involved therein, the client's words may carry special meanings which should be explored in the interview and often should be reproduced in the entry. The play interview with children calls for highly developed skill and is being studied so much that reproduction, in part at least, is essential. Process does not, however, in itself assure us that the affective quality will be grasped, and whenever the interaction does not make the emotional overtones self-evident, comment is desirable and even necessary.

## 5

## THE SUMMARY IS A GOOD DEVICE FOR ORGANIZING AND ANALYZING FACTS

Summaries, as already indicated, may be either recapitulated from already recorded material, or may be condensed from the worker's notebook. When the problem is deeply rooted in relationships, as expressed through emotionally charged conversation or as acted out in behavior, the interviewer or observer may want to reproduce a good deal of this moving, changing experience, and will be likely to use the narrative style, as shown in the preceding chapter. On the other hand, more static, objective facts may well be blocked and summarized. Also, whenever there are routine services, such as arrangements for use of a social resource, or uneventful periods of supervision, these periods of treatment may be economically and satisfactorily summarized. Interview material, process effect, may be treated the same way.

· TYPES OF SUMMARY

Summaries commonly found in records include: social histories, diagnostic summaries, periodic summaries, treatment evaluations, evaluation of a foster home, transfer summaries, closing entries, and also case abstracts from other records. In this chapter we shall discuss and illustrate only the more factual type of summary, reserving interpretative writing for later chapters.[1]

### Social Histories

Social histories are of two main kinds, with, however, many similar and overlapping features: the social-economic history

[1] See Chapters 6, on diagnosis, and 7, evaluation, following

perhaps most familiar in public assistance as an "eligibility" study; and the psycho-social or psycho-genetic history, familiar in clinics and child guidance agencies. Such studies or histories, which conform to some extent to a preconceived pattern of the relevant social situation, or the life experience, are commonly blocked under topics which reflect the agency's purposes. Young workers often make the mistake of assuming that because there is an outline or pattern in the office the interview must be taken under topics with question and answer. Another common error is to think that because an interview has followed a certain course, the recording should follow the same order. This should be clarified. Skill in *interviewing* determines how the interview is conducted; the style of *recording* is determined by the nature of the content, its place in the record; the use to be made of it by case workers; and other considerations.

Public assistance agencies make a pattern study of eligibility because of the legal framework within which grants are made. This pattern always gives evidence necessary in establishing need and, beyond that, such specific data as may be required by the various provisions of the act. Thus age, citizenship, marriage, degree of blindness or other disability, settlement, status in the armed forces (veterans), and so forth become not only items on application blanks but headings in an arranged study. Family composition, living arrangements, home management, financial and income data, relatives, are all part of the ordinary social situation which are likely to be recorded. Such data yield themselves readily to topical arrangement and make review of eligibility easier thereafter. There will be cases in which the personal and emotional reactions are so prominent, the interviewing process so important, that the slower moving narrative-chronological work-up may be preferred, but for most cases the topical summary is convenient. We should note, however, that the intake interview in public assistance, as in other agencies, usually is given in narrative style and for the same reasons.[2]

When the problem is one of behavior or psychoneurotic personality, or other psycho-social involvement, it is well known

[2]See p. 100 *et seq.*

that family relationships, particularly early family relationships, are important. Histories will stress parental background, including cultural conditioning, developmental history of the child or children, health, school, work and leisure-time activities, all important attitudes and relationships, also a careful account of the problem behavior, its beginnings, the areas in which it breaks out and toward whom it is directed. Financial and economic data will usually be included, but not given so prominent a place as in a financial need situation. It is good practice in such problems not to use too many explicit headings, since family relationships interact and summaries with over-refined classifications lead to repetition.

The following social study, topical arrangement, in a family agency record, is a condensation of four interviews with Mrs. F., telephone conversations with client, case worker in the day nursery, and medical social worker.

*Presenting Problem*

Mrs. Frank telephoned to request an immediate appointment. She said the Day Nursery was refusing to keep Tommy (aged 4) any longer and she has been forced to leave the child alone at home while she works. Tommy has been returned to his former foster mother for a temporary period.

The Down Town Day Nursery refused to keep Tommy because of his excessive demands for the teacher's attention, which disrupted the group. Mrs. Frank's description of the nursery problem was poor eating, fighting with other children, fussing at nap time. Tommy suffered two periods of illness during his short stay in nursery school, with two periods of hospitalization advised by the school physician.

The conversation with the day nursery indicated that the difficulties emanated from the mother's handling, which was inconsistent and punitive. The worker was provoked with Mrs. F. because she didn't follow suggestions made to her about the handling of the child.

*Mrs. F.'s Attitude toward the Problem*

Mrs. Frank started by saying that she hates to admit it, but she has a "problem child." She tried in every way to make a good home for him but he will not cooperate. She states, as though seeking the case worker's approval, that everyone has been wonderful to them, but

Tommy is willfully uncooperative. As an example, she points out that the nurses in the hospital found him intolerable. (Discussion later with the medical worker revealed that whereas Tommy's behavior is attention seeking, he was considered troublesome in the hospital primarily because of the nursing shortage.)

She feels that he deliberately procrastinates with food to make her late to work. Handling of the feeding problem has been in terms of punishment, depriving him of deserts, spanking him, and putting him to bed, all yielding equally ineffective results. She thinks the child needs rigid discipline and that he takes advantage of kindness. In her discussion she refers to the child as a "brat."

She explained her decision not to place Tommy in another foster home (her request at application earlier) in terms of feeling she should make a home for him. She wanted to prove she was strong and could assume obligations.

*Family Situation*

Mrs. Frank has been separated for six months from her husband, a Navy man. She planned to separate from him before when he was shipped out one and one-half years ago, but said nothing to him so as to receive support from him. They had lived apart periodically, Mrs. F. explaining this on the basis of difficulty in finding living quarters, her foster mother's need for her care, her husband's love affairs.

Mr. F. has recently received a medical discharge after a period of several month's hospitalization. He returned to his home town. Mrs. F. has refused to join him recently at his request, feeling that he should come if he wants to be with her. She likes her apartment and has a lease. There has been a succession of bickerings since he returned ill from India. She refused to join him at the naval hospital because she was working. She offered to join him later on, but he felt he wished to think it over. She felt humiliated by this and determined to refuse to rejoin him. He wants her only as a "woman," which she resents. She feels he wants her to wait on him and work for him now that he is sick.

Mr. F. sends $35 a month for Tommy's support. She resents his non-support and feels he should have shared the savings he brought back. She thinks the only contribution he could make to the family would be to discipline the boy.

She thinks their difficulties are due to their difference in background, she being a city girl and he a country boy. Her lips curl scornfully as she talks of her husband, and her tone is derisive. She resorts to mockery when she quotes him.

## Mother's Background

Mrs. F. came from a Jewish family. Her mother's health was poor after her birth, and she died when the child was sixteen months old, leaving Mrs. F. to a Gentile neighbor who had befriended her. Her only sibling, a girl seven years her senior, lived with the father. Mrs. F. expressed a verbal acceptance of this on the basis of her sister's age, but talks in a hostile tone about her sister as well as her father, who she feels mistreated her mother. She violently rejects Judaism, her father's religion, and arranged a non-Jewish burial for him last year when he died. She was severely criticized for this by her father's relatives, but stated defensively that she cannot know the ways of a religion in which she was not raised. After she had placed Tommy, she lived in her father's home until his death.

Mrs. F. was married at the age of eighteen, after five dates with her husband. She knew him only as "Slim," meeting him on a double date. He seemed a "perfect gentleman," and since he was stationed in the West, this seemed to be her life's dream coming true. To case worker's comment that the dream had not lasted, Mrs. F. expressed herself as being a person who does not waste time in regrets. One of her friends remarried three times before she found the proper husband, and she will do the same, if necessary. She is determined about one thing, not to have any more children.

The marriage experience was romantic at first when they were carefree, having good times. However, her husband's idea of a good time was to visit bars and amuse his friends with cheap jokes. She preferred to go out less frequently in better style. Then he decided she should settle down and take responsibility. She took responsibility and he shed his. She assumed all the responsibility for Tommy while her husband had a good time.

She lived with her own foster mother after Tommy's birth, joining her husband intermittently for short periods. They set up their first home when Tommy was sixteen months old. Mr. F. had several love affairs, according to his wife, and requested a divorce each time to marry the love of his life. She refused because she recognized he was subject to passing fancies.

Mrs. F. was employed as a secretary for a publishing company. She spoke of herself as one meant to be a "career woman" and as very competent on the job. However, she soon reported she had resigned her job, projecting the blame upon Tommy, whom she had to take to clinic during his frequent illnesses.

Her vocational history indicates only short sequences of employment. Before her marriage she worked for only brief periods on a variety of jobs to have money for luxuries. After marriage, because of her husband's low rating in the Navy and small salary, she worked occasionally when she wanted something special. Mr. F. objected to her working and leaving Tommy, and Mrs. F. resented his attitude. After Tommy was placed with Mrs. Y., Mrs. F. worked, using her money for clothes, since she only paid her father five dollars weekly for board and received one hundred dollars a month from her husband.

Mrs. F. objects to routine jobs such as the one she held with a government agency for a short time. Although she found herself educationally unsuited for the job at the publishing house and lost it after three weeks, she still wants a "real secretarial job" with a publishing company because she wants to meet important people and make something of herself. She wants a five-day-a-week job, with salary sufficient to pay $42 a month rent. She prefers working for a man because they are more sympathetic than women.

## History of Child

The child was born three years after his parent's marriage when Mr. Frank thought it was time for his wife to settle down and mature. The child was always a feeding problem and regurgitated when "upset." When the case worker asked Mrs. F. what she meant by the child being upset, she simply related a story about one of her friends who forces her infant to eat eggs, causing the child to stiffen in resistance. She sees this as a portrayal of her own behavior with Tommy, who used to become rigid to resist forced feedings. He presented sleeping difficulties too, and cried until picked up from his crib. The Franks quarreled about the handling of the child. In elaboration of this point Mrs. F. was only able to see that her husband wanted her to treat Tommy "like a man."

Mrs. F. feels the early difficulties were due to Tommy's being spoiled by her father and her own foster mother, who felt it was bad for him to cry since he was a boy and might rupture himself.

At sixteen months of age, Tommy fell ill after an all-day shopping trip with his mother, who neglected to take him to the bathroom, resulting in the child wetting himself several times. He was in a naval hospital for four months, seriously ill, with bronchiactasis and resection of several ribs was considered. Mrs. F. feels his recurrent bronchial cough results from this illness. At present he coughs whenever food is presented.

The hospital reports him underweight and anemic.

## Foster Home Placement

Tommy was placed in the foster home when his father was assigned to overseas service. Mrs. F. went to live with her father and decided to go to work. She felt sorry for Mrs. Y., the foster mother, who, she states, was depressed because of the loss of a foster child "kidnapped" by his mother, and offered to permit Tommy to live with her. Mrs. F. visited frequently, buying Tommy expensive gifts.

## Behavior Observed at Home

Tommy awakened from his nap shortly after my home visit. He is a pale, colorless, pathetic-looking child. Mrs. F. presented his lunch to him explaining they had slept late because Tommy awakened during the air raid alert last night and was restless thereafter. She offered him a bowl of unattractive looking lentil soup, bread and butter, and a glass of milk. Tommy began to cough and his mother at once reprimanded him, at first mildly, but then in an increasingly shrill, sharp tone. The child began to gag and his mother hurried him to the bathroom, explaining she had taught him to spit up phlegm to avoid regurgitation. She discussed this in detail in the child's presence, trying to draw the case worker into a condemnation of his behavior. The scene culminated in Tommy's being sent to bed under threat of remaining there all day. He soon begged to return, offering to eat. Her manner was very critical and she talked in the same derisive tone she used when talking of her husband. She met his reluctance to eat by saying: "You don't like it, do you? It tastes bad when it's cold. You don't like it hot and you don't like it cold. How do you like it, on a silver platter?"

The child was quite responsive when I played with him for a few minutes. This conforms with the statement of the medical social worker about the child's responsiveness to her.

Later, mother used the convalescent opening punitively, threatening not to let Tommy go when he seemed eager to do so, since he had been "bad." While she stated her reluctance to let him go, when I said he might be away for only a month, she said, "Is that all?"

The eligibility study and the psychogenetic history will be distinguished only in emphasis, since, although the eligibility process is concerned with social and economic data primarily and the history, as the phrase implies, with attitudes, behavior, and relationhips, each may have some topics in common.

## Periodic Summaries

A social history covers the period of time antecedent to application; a periodic summary always refers to a period of time under care of the agency—a period of treatment; a summary of what occurred *between* applications is called an "interval," not a periodic summary. Periodic summaries are commonly: a topical review similar to the original eligibility study;[3] condensed straight narrative for periods of treatment and, more rarely, topical summaries for periods of treatment. In reviews of eligibility it is not necessary to repeat details which are unchanged, but to indicate only important changes in the picture.

Several variants of treatment summaries follow. First a long summary, which is, however, an economy as over against four separate interviews. Note that the material is condensed in "process" style.

*November, 1944.* During this month Mrs. C. talked more and more about the way she has been feeling about her husband. She was pleased because he sent her a pocketbook, but in the next sentence stated that he "had made arrangements" for her to get an extra $10 allotment and she would believe it when she saw it.

I discussed how hard it was for her to believe that he was really trying to do things for her and make a go of the Army. Although some things had happened to annoy her and she was upset when he didn't write regularly, still he had been made a corporal. He had sent her this present and he wrote regularly. It could almost seem as though every time he did something nice she thought of something else for him to prove. She picked this up—that was quite true—she really has no faith in him and never has had. She never did believe the things he told her about getting along well until it was absolutely proved. Although time after time he's had no trouble getting a job she never would believe it until he brought home his first week's pay. Even if he

[3]See p. 97 for discussion in public assistance.

went out every day at a regular time she still wouldn't believe that he had a new job until she saw the pay check.

As though she were considering the idea for the first time—maybe that has been the whole trouble with her marriage—that she hasn't had faith in him. She would nag at him and he would get annoyed. It was because she was so afraid he would disappoint her. Worker suggested that sometimes people bring on the things they are afraid of as though they couldn't believe that things could go well. She agreed. She guessed it is because she has always been disappointed in people. It started out with her mother—that is the primary reason for her never believing in anybody; that her mother failed her. If a child in its early youth starts out having been let down by his mother it's hard to ever get over that feeling about everyone else they need or are close to. It's as though since her mother let her down she expects everybody else to. If she had had a mother who loved her and really wanted her, she thinks she would have felt different about other people. I agreed that feeling about her mother would certainly condition her feeling about other people, and it seemed hard to get over; she felt it was her lot in life always to be turned down and have a difficult time, so she just drove people to treating her that way. She said that was so.

I suggested, however, that because this had happened to her as a child did not mean it had to continue—her husband hadn't really let her down completely in the past, yet she herself had agreed their quarrels had driven him to doing things he might not have done otherwise. His going into the Army seemed pretty bad to her at the time, and yet now he's making every effort to show her that it will be a good thing for all of them. It will be easier for him to do well if she can encourage him some and let him see that she believes in his accomplishments. She agreed—said she had written him a nice letter when he sent her the present and told him how pleased she was. She supposed that he really couldn't afford any more or he would have sent something to the children, but again she wants him to think of everything.

During this month she complained of stomach pains. She was always afraid that her ulcer condition might return. She had been quite sick before marriage. She'd been on a very strict diet and had to be very careful. However, ever since she has been married she has been able to eat anything and has had no pains. Recently she's been so tied down looking after the children and has felt badly. We agreed she should have a physical check-up. She talked with some nostalgia of the time when her husband had a gas service station out in a small town. She loved working at the service station, meeting people, and being busy outdoors. She had much less responsibility for the children because there was a girl who could look out for them afternoons. If it hadn't been for the war and for her third pregnancy they might still be there. She agreed to my comments that the children always seem to have made things much more complicated for her. Her husband wanted children and she guesses that is really the reason she had them —the happiest kind of life for her would have been to just keep on working and doing things with her husband. She said this without showing a strong feeling of resentment, but rather in a wondering tone of voice as though it was again something she had not thought of before. She and her husband used to go out to a party every Saturday night and left a neighbor girl with the children. Although it was definitely her husband's business and he did all the planning and made the decisions, still he talked everything over with her. He always told her that she had good ideas. I said she sounded as though it gave her a lot of pleasure to have her husband pick up her ideas and to be working with him on things connected with the business. She did like it very much, even though she made it clear that it was really his business and she was more or less a silent partner.

At the end of the month she had a letter from her husband saying that he was taking exams for promotion. He was very happy about being recommended for this. She does hope that he gets his commission. I discussed with her the possibility that he might not get it. Perhaps she would then have some feeling of his having failed her. She said the exams were very tough and a lot of men do fail them. It would not be to his discredit if he didn't pass, and she really did believe that he was studying hard and doing his best.

Next a topical treatment summary, which condenses 7 office interviews and 5 telephone conversations with a young unmarried mother, 1 home visit, 4 collateral conferences, and 10 collateral telephone conversations. The writer believes that more effective selection and condensation would have been achieved had the worker not tried to follow topics. But here it can be argued that the health, educational, and other clearly defined services can easily be arranged in this manner. In all interviewing treatment the crux of the matter is that if the interview is skillfully and consciously directed the movement is *inherent.* Condensation, selection and comment by the worker are usually the most effective; rearrangement is unnecessary.

### Summary June-August

HEALTH.—Clara attended eye clinic regularly, for which we referred her to a specialist. He gave her considerable reassurance about use of her eyes for studying, definitely recommended a change of glasses, referred her to an optician who gave her a very reasonable rate. He discussed with her very frankly the situation in regard to her eyes, which she appreciated. She seemed considerably reassured by this visit and found the new glasses helpful. She went back for recheck on 8/24 since she had been feeling eyestrain, but he found her eyes still much improved.

WORK.—Clara continued as nursemaid a day or two a week throughout June; was paid for this at the rate of 50c an hour. She loved the little boy; had little difficulty in handling him; grew quite attached to the family, talked with them a great deal about her own home, the farm, the animals, etc. Although Clara liked this job she felt she had to get full-time employment which would pay her much more. (We suspected considerable financial pressure from Rachel.) Decided she would like to work in a drug store. The wages here were $22 a week plus tips, so she usually cleared at least $30 a week. She found the work tiring, but not too much so, seemed quite excited to be earning so much money. She kept this job for 5 weeks, but during this period did not have adequate rest or recreation; earned in all about $150 on this job. . . .

SCHOOL.—Clara showed a great deal of anxiety around her school work; studied very hard during June in preparation for the regents. She was very much afraid of failure; found the contents of the courses pretty overwhelming. We discussed with Clara the facts that the content was much stiffer than that she had known in her own school, that the other students in the courses probably had a much better preparation for it than she, that she had started three months after the other students, had to catch up, and also that she had been through a physical and emotional experience which necessarily had taken a great deal of her energy and strength. She was very much upset and ashamed of her grades; said no one in her family had ever had such grades and she questioned whether she ought to let any member of her family know exactly what her grades were. We said Clara had every right to be proud of having passed the history courses; thought that under the circumstances she had done exceedingly well. Clara responded eagerly to this, but did feel that she should have done much better. In her reaction to the cramming and her disappointment in the scores she made on the tests, she suddenly hated school, sold the books which she had originally loved so much, felt for a while she simply could not face the summer courses, didn't want to go to school again at all, did not see how she could live through it. We interpreted this as a natural way for Clara to react since it had been such a costly struggle for her, but encouraged her to try the summer courses, anticipating that she might feel a little differently after she had recovered from the strain of the regents. Clara's period of hating school did not last long, and she did enroll for French and algebra in the evening classes for the summer session. . . .

BABY.—Clara visited her baby regularly once a month. . . . She expressed her resentment against the foster mother, against both the adoptive agency and us, because of our participation in the plan for the adoption, against the potential adoptive parents. Clara seemed quite comfortable as she discussed the negative feelings, said she guessed she would hate anybody who helped her in her plans to have the baby adopted—of course did not know what she would have done without us. She realized that all of us had helped her a great deal, repeated that adoption was the only solution she could see for herself and the baby. We discussed the difference between Clara's thoughts and her feelings, knew that with her mind she realized this, but this did not mean at the same time she did not resent and dislike the people who were helping her to do the very things she had asked for, namely arrange for the adoption of her baby. We related this to the conflict in Clara herself, namely that part of her wanted to keep the baby, part of her knew it was best to give her up. Clara responded to this by discussing very freely her ambivalent feelings toward adoptive parents, but expressed positive feelings toward the agencies and case workers; said she guessed she always would feel sort of mixed up about the adoptive parents because they would have her baby. . . .

A summary in straight narrative condensation of five interviews with a boy at Children's Court, including one interview with his mother:

D. came in regularly during this period and continued to discuss his fears of basal metabolism, his activities, and his summer plans. He had broken another appointment for a B.M. and again he brought out

his fears. He wants to go through with it. When I told him that I had
also had it done to me he relaxed a great deal. I drew a diagram of the
set-up for him and he asked many intelligent questions. He took the
diagram with him. He felt that if he would be able to finally keep his
appointment, he would want to go alone, and rejected the offer of his
mother's or my accompanying him. The fear he articulated the most
was that he would have to take his clothes off. It seemed to indicate
to him that he would no longer have control of the situation. We discussed how he was brave in other situation, e.g., the job he held at the
carnival where he could easily be hit by the ball. He finally kept his
appointment, was afraid when he went down, but soon realized he
would not be hurt. He was mighty glad to get it over with. He seemed
to have observed it all very carefully because he corrected some of my
descriptions of the machine. I asked what his mother had said when he
came home. He said she praised him just like I am doing. The doctor
explained to him that there is nothing—his development is just a little
slow, but normal. He is happy that everything is all right. He was put
on a diet and at first thought he would be able to follow it, but the
next week said he couldn't. He likes to eat too much and since there
isn't anything wrong with him he doesn't care that he is a little over-
weight. He doesn't pay attention to the boys if they call him any
names, and so they soon stop. I used this to get into a discussion of
how he must really want to do something before he can go through
with it. I recalled when he first started coming to the clinic how he
felt he could stop stealing because the judge told him to, and he could
go on a diet if a doctor recommended it. But a person in authority
cannot always make one change unless one wants to. He is not able to
follow the diet because he doesn't want to, and he could stop stealing
because he himself wanted to stop. The judge may have given him the
first desire to control himself, but to continue controlling himself has
to come from within him. He thought that was true—that he had
gotten into trouble and decided it wasn't worth it. Besides, he has no
desire or urge to steal any more. He can go in the neighborhood where
he used to steal and not think of stealing.

School is better. His father was asked to come to school and he is
now helping D. with his homework. We discussed the possibility of D.
getting extra homework as an aid to his better understanding of arith-
metic. He followed my suggestion and asked his teacher to give him
extra homework.

At first he wanted to go to camp, and then when he learned of the possibility of farm work he preferred that, because he would be away the entire summer. He is going to get his working papers so he can get some odd jobs if he wishes to.

Next, sharply condensed single-entry topical summaries for a medical chart:[4]

### Vacation Arranged for Patient

SUMMER, 1939.—At the doctor's request, we assisted Mrs. Berger in arranging to go to the Saratoga Spa for a vacation of three weeks to complete a course of treatment there. She did very well while she was away from home, and said that she felt extremely well. She talked a good deal about the town and her association with other patients, apparently made one or two friends. After her report of the summer, she stopped in only occasionally to see us and to let us know that she was continuing to have difficulty in managing on her budget, in spite of her move to a new apartment.

### Attempt to Help the Patient Budget Her Income

Patient has talked about her budget always in terms of needing more money either from her daughter or from the worker. She has felt, however, that she cannot keep asking her daughter for more money, because the daughter threatens to leave home, and then Mrs. Berger will be left alone. She has thought about splitting up her home and trying to get a furnished room by herself, getting support from Home Relief, but she realizes this would probably be possible only if she made quite a break with her daughter.

Patient reviewed her spending spasmodically with us. From the list she brought us, it appeared that she marketed quite well. She had the habit, however, of spending money when she had it, and not laying it aside for rent, etc., so that she ran short by purchasing a few more extras than she could afford. When this was pointed out to her she accepted her habit more or less as inevitable, saying that there were so many things she needed that it was very difficult, and she did not think she could change her method very much.

### Vacation-Rest at Saratoga Spa

SUMMER, 1940.—We again arranged Spa treatments for Mrs. Berger. The doctor felt that if she could get away again with a little more lift,

[4]See pp. 107–111.

she might possibly be able to undertake some form of employment, as her condition has continued to improve, although her complaints have not improved equally. Mrs. Berger did not feel so well when she returned home. For her summer expense she was allowed $38 from the Social Service Arthritis Fund. It was arranged that her daughter should pay for her carfare to Saratoga. Mrs. Berger admitted that she enjoyed being away from home some of the time, and on her return said that she was quite sure that having a job would be of some help to her.

### Attempts to Find Employment

FALL, 1940.—Mrs. Berger herself tried during the fall of 1940 to find a job, and made application to one of the local movie houses to act as a matron during afternoon shows. She also applied to the city for this sort of job. She investigated the Exchange for Part-Time Work for Women, but found that they could only offer her clerical work, for which she was not fitted. She looked around at various other places trying to find a place through friends, but was not successful in any of these attempts.

After going herself to the Central Office of the Knights of Pythias, she asked that we bring her case to their attention, which we did by visit and letter of interpretation. . . .

Next, condensation of interview material, process effect, in periodic summary.

At the interview following the psychiatric conference, Mrs. Gerber came in with many complaints about the child and reports of her own handling, which was obviously very destructive. I took up with her quite directly the effect upon the child of this kind of handling, his constant need to retaliate against her, and the fact that he is able to adjust to a different kind of handling, in school, in the street, and in interviews with his case worker. I gave sufficient recognition to the fact that disturbance within her and the lack of gratification in her own life made it extremely difficult for her to put up with normal kind of behavior in a child, and to handle herself in a consistent manner with him. Mrs. G. was at first very defensive, but as I discussed with her her loneliness, and her expectations of Isaac, she became more accepting of the criticisms I made and admitted that she knew that even though she disagreed with me, I was trying to help her.

In subsequent interviews there seemed to be a very definite change in her attitude toward me and in her use of our time together. We focused more and more on the sources of her own unhappiness. When she complained about the difficulties she was having with Isaac, I pointed out to her her inability to take any steps that would remedy the situation, such as her inability to send him to an afternoon play school, her refusal to move from her mother, her unwillingness to go to work, etc. It is also interesting to note that after this interview there were fewer complaints about her itching. It definitely seemed to be getting better.

After I had proposed alternatives very directly to Mrs. Gerber, she thought about it for a while and then came back to say that she decided to let nature take its course. Maybe her mother will marry and then leave the home. When I questioned whether she really believes that this would happen she admitted that her mother will probably not get married again. However, she will wait and see. Maybe Isaac will change. She definitely could not face placement in an afternoon play school, saying that he would be indoors, and by this I was able to illustrate to her her need to be constantly entangled with the child, her inability to let him go, and the kind of negative gratification she gets from this.

While she has now enough security with me to bear some of this discussion, her resistance to change is so great and her rationalizations so strong, that I did not feel much progress was made during this period.

In the above illustration, note the sentence or two of evaluation which provides an additional short cut.

## Transfer Summary

Next to closing entries, "transfer summaries" enjoy a certain popularity. Indeed, a summary may be written only when the case is to be transferred to another district or worker. While this is better than to have no summary at all, summaries *should* be written as needed and not merely when an administrative event forces them. They should be written by the worker who has been carrying the case. Although it is perfectly possible to write a case abstract on a closed case or one not otherwise known to us, a more dynamic summary is made by one who knows first hand the case dynamics. Since transfer summaries in content should conform to their appropriate purpose—social history, diagnosis, treatment, evaluation—it is not necessary to illustrate all these variations. Transfer summaries should not be merely case "abstracts." A special feature in any instance of intensive treatment would be to describe or comment on the client's preparation for change of worker at transfer and his reactions.

## The Closing Entry

One of the oldest types of summary is the so-called "closing entry." It should focus on the *course and results of treatment*, and not on social study material or on diagnosis, although outstanding problems may be mentioned. We are interested at this point in accounting for the progress of the client while under care. The closing entry may run from the simple statement "man at work," or "family moved" (a mere note as to the reason for closing the case), to a short paragraph covering the following points: situation at intake and persons involved; problems emerging; services or treatment given; progress, movement, or change; results and status on closing. Sometimes significant events in the life of the family while under care but not as affected by treatment, are also included, and sometimes a forecast, in the event of reopening, is added.

Two closing entries from a family agency and a medical social department, respectively, follow:

## Closing Entry

Mrs. M. applied for assistance on 3/3/35, having been referred by the Emergency Relief Administration. She was ineligible to receive assistance from that agency because she did not meet their residence requirements. She was old enough for an old age assistance grant but could not get proof of her age or residence. There was an acute financial need, since she had exhausted all the resources that she had had after her husband's death. Her chief concern was to try to secure damages and subsequent royalties from a cotton cleaning process invented and patented by her husband, which was being used illegally by numerous cotton concerns. She appeared to be a very intelligent but slightly eccentric old lady, highly suspicious and very active.

Three main lines of treatment have been followed: financial relief was given to her in the form of rent only, since her friends would provide food. She seemed to have a feeling of security in this and to understand that she could always request other assistance if she needed it. Much time was spent in trying to learn something of the legal problem concerning the cotton cleaning process. An effort was made to evaluate her prospects of receiving financial return and to inquire into the standing of the lawyers and interested parties assisting her in this litigation. There seems to be little question that she has a real case and at the present time the indications are that a lawyer, who is working directly with her, is an honest and intelligent person and can be relied upon to guide her wisely. Considering that the possibility of financial returns from the patent appeared very indefinite and hazy, it seemed advisable to help her in making a plan for regular support. She was referred to the Division of Old Age, and help was given her in establishing her age and residence. She was granted assistance from that agency amounting to $33.00 monthly on 3/1/37.

Now that she has competent advice and guidance regarding her patent affairs and is assured of a regular source of income until such time as she may secure some returns from the patent, there seems to be no further need for service.

Date closed 3/31/37. (Stamp)

## Closing Entry

This patient, a 30-year-old widow of Italian parentage, was referred in February, 1939, to Social Service for financial assistance in obtaining arch supports. Diagnoses were rheumatoid arthritis since 1928, psoriasis, obesity, and diabetes melitus. She was being supported by cousins who could meet only her subsistence needs. Up to the time of our contact, she had had a very protected life. Her husband had died in September, 1938, leaving her without any means of subsistence, and she had to depend on relatives. A great disappointment in her life was that her adopted son had turned out to be feeble-minded and had to be placed in a state school. When we became acquainted with her, she was depressed, anxious, and felt extremely helpless.

During our three-year contact the patient was seen every one or two months on an average. We assisted her financially to procure extras which her relatives could not supply, to the amounts of $5.50 for arch supports; $25 for clothing; $10 for training as a beautician (not completed), and $47 for a three weeks stay at the Spa. This stay appeared to have been especially beneficial in the patient's eyes and during it she lost eight pounds, bringing her down to the lowest weight since we have known her. Arthritic pains and psoriasis, which had gradually improved during 1940 and 1941, were considerably improved at this time, much to the patient's satisfaction. Patient consistently showed need to discuss her conflict over her adopted son, and seemed gradually to come to accept more his being in an institution. Toward the end of our contact, in December, 1941, she discussed some unsatisfactory aspects of living with her cousins, and of attending the clinic where she was unable to obtain free insulin. She then changed her home to live with a sister. She might later go to housekeeping with her mother if they were eligible for Home Relief. She understood that if need arose, she could get in touch with us. Since she did not expect, however, to need our assistance in clinic, we are discontinuing the case. 1-22-42.

Like the transfer summary, the closing entry originally had an administrative purpose, namely, as a convenience in making reports to enquiring agencies. A closing entry need not be longer than a paragraph or two, and narrative, rather than topical style, seems to be the most satisfactory. Most people agree that this brief analysis of stewardship is an important professional, self-supervisory tool, but the place for detailed evaluation of treatment is not at closing unless the case is technically interesting and likely to be used for study by staff or students. If it is expected that the case will be reopened, fuller closing entries, which thus take on the character of treatment evaluations are justified.

### · SUMMARY

Summary is an excellent device for the recapitulation of facts. Organizing material is a discipline in analysis: it helps us to think about significant relationships; it assists us to formulate trends; it economizes not only time spent in reading the record, but usually the time spent aimlessly with the client. Both topical and narrative summaries are useful, the former largely for periods of study, and the latter for treatment. Even intensive therapy, making full use of worker-client relationship, can be held in notes and reduced effectively in process style. We must remind ourselves of the limitations inherent in summary—the tendency toward oversimplification, toward oversharp outlines when the life process is fluid and shapeless, the danger of obscuring sequences and possibly of blurring the emotional overtones in behavior and verbalizing. Sources of information should be indicated in study summaries, and care should be taken to bring out client reactions in periodic summaries. Some of the disadvantages of summary in emotional material are met when workers have sufficient skill to introduce diagnostic and evaluation comment, as we shall see in the next chapters.

# 6

# GOOD THINKING IS ESSENTIAL TO GOOD RECORDING

EVEN THOUGH A RECORD HAVE A SUFFICIENCY OF FACT, it is not professionally an adequate tool unless it also contains the worker's thinking about the facts, or interpretation. Supervisors and social scientists have been heard to say "give us an accurate reproduction of the facts and we will judge for ourselves." In training, this may be a necessary step but, by and large, the competent worker who knows the facts at first hand is in the best position to interpret them. Consultation may assist, but cannot relieve the worker of his obligation to think about the meaning of the request, the behavior, and the case as a whole.

## · THE DIAGNOSTIC PROCESS

The word *diagnosis* means thorough understanding, and although the term has been pre-empted by medicine, actually it is a good Greek word susceptible of general application, until some better term is invented. As used in social work, it means not only understanding the problem, but the person who has the problem. Diagnosis is a professional opinion about the real nature of the problem the client presents. To answer the question "What is the matter?" is difficult. Workers would rather think a diagnostic answer than say it, would rather say it than write it down. They are afraid of labeling, afraid to be wrong, fancy they don't know. Yet if they treat the case at all they must consciously or unconsciously, written or unwritten, act on a diagnostic hypothesis. We must have tentative hypotheses in order to conduct even a first interview with any sense of direction, but a hypothesis isn't much good unless it is clearly formulated.

Workers say, "Won't it do if I have it in my head?" No, it won't do. Since a diagnosis is always tentative, we should not be afraid to record it early, certainly within the first three or four contacts. It is progressively less useful the longer one puts it off. A diagnosis may be adequate for the specific treatment objective; it may be proved wrong; it may be refined or modified by deeper understanding. The important thing is to make and record it early and revise it as often as may be necessary, for the diagnostic process is merely a form of "methodical guess work."

Does not the actual recording of a diagnostic statement perhaps inhibit thinking? May not the worker say, "Well, now I have done my thinking," when after all he has merely indulged in a few descriptive generalizations and stereotypes? Yes, this is entirely possible, but it is less likely if the worker has achieved the kind of diagnostic habit which underpins interpretation with the specific detail. The remedy for loose thinking is not *less* thinking, but *more* thinking, and the remedy for hasty and inaccurate generalization lies in the habit of repeated diagnostic attempts and of case analysis through staff discussion. Workers who have formed the habit of putting their thinking together about the meaning of the case are likely to develop professional skill faster than those who have not.

The meaning of a total case in its purest sense would include all the significant positive, as well as the negative, factors. Concurrently with the defining of the problem, the worker is also appraising the client's capacity to deal with his problems, his strengths, his resources, his accessibility to treatment. That is, we must think not only of the problem and its causes, but of the client's potentialities for solving his problem. This appraisal is one of evaluation. Because the diagnostic movement and the evaluation movement interweave in our thinking, and may be written down on the same page or even in the same paragraph, does not mean that they are the same intellectual discipline. Both diagnosis and evaluation are involved in a thorough understanding of the case. Evaluation is part of the larger dynamic whole. Nevertheless, the writer believes that to acquire facility in the diagnostic defining process as such helps the worker to relate and base his evaluation more adequately. Students say, can I not use a "mixed" form of diagnosis and evaluation? Well, mixed it will be unless and until they have thoroughly mastered the concept of accurate diagnosis in its narrower sense.

Diagnosis is particularly complicated in social case work because it is not only the problem but a configuration of person who has the problem, or who is reacting to his problem. A person may have a problem somewhat external to him, as when we say he has "insufficient" income due to low wages, due to the fact that his industry doesn't pay good wages; or he may be more involved in his problem causally when his anxiety and hostility get him into "jams" which make him less valuable to the company, and in either case he will have attitudes toward or reactions to his situation which are all part of the dynamics of diagnosis. Moreover, typically, a social case work diagnosis is interpersonal—"the child's problem, temper tantrums, are a reaction to rejection by his mother." Social diagnosis is usually a cycle of cause and effect phenomena, either person to situation, or person to person, or both.

### · FORMS OF DIAGNOSIS

The diagnostic attempt is found in the record under such captions as: *problem, diagnostic summary, diagnostic statement,* or less formally under "worker's impression" or *interpretation;* also *diagnostic conference.* In his application the client locates his problem in some fashion. Even at intake we have to have some preliminary notion of what his problem seems to be in order to determine whether he should be treated in this agency or referred elsewhere. A person comes to us because he is suffering from some dislocation in his social functioning or social adjustment which he could not, or thought he could not, work out for himself. The trouble may largely originate in external factors, or the trouble may be, and indeed often is, a combination of internal strains and external pressures. The diagnostic process describes and defines. Since definition gains in precision and accuracy by giving the causes of the problem, we may say that the diagnostic process inherently strives toward causal explanation.

Thus, we might say that "state of unemployment" is a descriptive and defining phrase, but it is not, in itself, precise. If we add to this:

This man is unemployed because his technical hand-skilled operation has been mechanized, and his rigid personality structure has made it particularly hard for him to change to another trade

we have a clearer picture of person and problem interaction. Again, to examine a descriptive definition like "sibling rivalry." As it stands, this is a good enough label for classification purposes, but we get a better sense of causality when we say:

In this case of sibling rivalry the problem has been aggravated by the fact that John was an only child, much loved and petted for five years. With the birth of the baby, Frank, not only was he unprepared for the baby's coming, but Frank's succession of early illnesses so completely disrupted the household and took the attention away from John, that he had the experience over a long period of being completely neglected and rejected.

## Problem Classification

This is the simplest form of diagnosis. In classification we cannot easily show causality; we index only the main problems, with no attempt to give the minutiae and subtle differences which make each case unlike every other case. Whenever we want to show how unlike a case is to a type, we must use some sort of diagnostic statement; whenever we want to show likeness to the type, we must classify. It is not enough to look at happenings in the order in which they take place in human experience; things must be classified according to their essential nature. Unlike physicians, who use the label form of diagnosis—for example, tuberculosis—social case workers rarely use classification of problems in the case record. Many agencies use a check list of diagnostic labels on a Kardex, which may be used for statistical and other purposes. The writer would prefer to find these formal classifications also used in the record itself, not as a substitute for, but in addition to, diagnostic statement. As a matter of fact, stating the main problems somewhere in a record is a good habit to acquire. Many problem classifications are in com-

mon use in case work, for example, unemployment, insufficient
income, sibling rivalry, conduct disorder, primary behavior
problems, marital difficulty, alcoholism, unmarried mother,
child born out of wedlock, rejection, desertion, non-support,
crippled child, and so on. Such diagnostic phrases come to have
more meaning when linked together with the interrelationships
shown, as in a diagnostic statement (below), but the naming of
the problem is a help in early focusing.

### Diagnostic Summaries

These are similar to social study or social history summaries
described earlier[1]—the diagnostic effect deriving largely from
the topical arrangement with, perhaps, interpretative comment.
Sometimes a social history is followed by a diagnostic paragraph
and treatment plan, the whole called "diagnostic summary."
Child guidance clinics often use this type of summary in preparation for conference. The headings might be: problem presented,
developmental history, parental background, relationships and
behavior, medical and psychological examination, diagnostic
statement, treatment goals. Diagnostic summaries are sometimes used in referring a case to another agency, the amount of
factual material being helpful when one does not see the record
itself. Sometimes a full interpretation of each person in the
family is also called a diagnostic summary. We should remember
that the distinguishing characteristic of social diagnosis is that
it is interpersonal—husband-wife; parent-child; sibling. Unlike
medicine, social case work does not typically have a "patient"
diagnosis. See next illustration for interpersonal type:

### Diagnostic Summary

The problem is that of anxiety and depression in a Greek Orthodox
family related to the desertion of the wife, the man's illness apparently
being precipitated by his wife's renewing relations with a former lover.
The advent of a rival seems to have touched off the entire range of
patient's insecurity, which spread from the sexual into all areas of patient's functioning, and resulted in the present breakdown. At present,

[1]See Chapter 5 and p. 86.

patient seems to feel that his total security rests on his being able to exhibit sexual prowess before his wife.

The man's lack of ego strength seems to be explained in part by his attachment to an aggressive, domineering mother and, in part, to his small stature, of which he is ashamed. We know of no heterosexual ties until patient became attached to his wife. She has physical attributes which patient would easily associate with "glamorous femininity." Possibly her attraction for patient was influenced by the ego-supportive value which such an alliance would have, especially for a person who is so insecure regarding his own sexuality. Evidence of anxiety with respect to his potency was reflected in patient's need to have intercourse several times a day during this early period of his marriage.

Wife appears to be an immature person in her inability to be realistic about personal relationships, or to take responsibility for situations which she gets into, and for decisions in regard to the direction of her life.

We see indications of early maladjustment in wife's relationship to parents. The father, too old and ill to show interest in his children, was a very stern, rigidly demanding man, who exercised a strong restrictive influence in the home. Wife's later life adjustments reflect the pattern which was set up in reaction to this early situation—namely, ambivalence in wanting to rebel, but being unable to carry the rebellion through without conflict, and in returning to conformity.

At adolescence, when first experimenting with heterosexual contacts, she became involved in intimate relations with a married man, her senior by ten years. This relationship represented rebellion against her family and their cultural codes. At the age of twenty-one, she made a second attempt to escape from the restricting demands of her family circle. This time, she chose a conforming way of escape—betrothal and marriage to a man of similar background and faith. From this, as from her original familial setting, she sought escape by a renewal of the first attachment. Unable again to carry this through without conflict, she returned once more to conformity by setting up housekeeping with her mother and seeking companionship in girl friends. Now she is in conflict as to whether she should resume her marriage.

## Diagnostic Statement

A short form of diagnosis, with the factual evidence reduced and subordinated to the interpretation, is called a diagnostic statement. The phrase was first used by M. Antoinette Cannon in connection with medical social practice. This form is particularly suitable when recording must be as compact as possible, for example, in a unit medical social record, but it is also a good working form for the practitioner with an average case load in which he wants to keep the diagnostic element realistic and the recording not too burdensome. Diagnostic statements, because of their simplicity, may occur at not infrequent intervals as new problems emerge or understanding deepens.

In practicing this sort of interpretation, it is helpful to make a scratch paper list of "findings," or important factors in the case, for instance:

Young Greek widow with two children living at home.

Exhaustion of insurance and savings leaves them without resources, except for relatives who supervise her activities.

Woman had a hard life of drudgery prior to her happy marriage.

Husband died in explosion, leaving woman pregnant with second child.

Elder child, aged 7, Irene, has temper tantrums, abuses her sister, and is hard to discipline at home and at school. She has IQ of 130.

Posthumously born child, aged 4, extremely delicate, has called for mother's attention from birth.

Relatives oppose woman working out of home, so she is much with the children.

Woman is affectionate with children and intelligent. Embroiders beautifully and is eager to learn what she "does to Irene" to make her so bad.

Findings are to diagnosis as ingredients are to a pudding. Findings are not something in addition to diagnosis. Diagnosis is the meaning derived from all the significant elements, but particularly the negative elements which comprise the problem. Findings are both positive and negative. The balance between positive and negative elements gives us evaluation.

In order to make a diagnosis out of such raw materials, or "findings," we have to focus, weight, and interrelate them differently, depending on whether the request was for financial assistance, nursery school care, or something else, as one cannot effectively diagnose in the abstract. But focusing in an arbitrary fashion we might say:

This is the case of a Greek widow's child, whose temper tantrums and aggressive behavior at home and at school are, in part, a reaction to an intense rivalry situation with a younger sister, to whom the mother's attention is constantly directed both because of her delicacy and because she is the last "pledge" of a much loved husband. The mother's restricted life and cultural habits keep her within the home circle, and the interest of relatives, although a potential resource, is over-dominating. Exhaustion of savings makes the family financially dependent. The mother's manual skill, general intelligence, and capacity for insight, and the superior intelligence and vigor of the child herself, suggest a favorable outcome.

Note that the last sentence is prognostic, or shows the complementary evaluation process, which will be discussed later. [2]

Or conversely, for practice, let us take an example of "pure" interpretation and fill in the findings from an imagined social history:

This is the case of an adolescent boy (age) living at home (describe family situation) with severe restrictions on all normal activities (describe) due to crippling congenital disease (medical report). Criticized and complained of by his parents (give details), who have completely rejected him from birth (how), he reacts to them and to all other relationships (what) with marked resentment, hostility, inability to accept any limitations (give details of reaction), and by projection of blame on the world (what does he say).

In this way we learn how more specific interpretation can be given, if desired, through the introduction of supporting findings. A handful of diagnostic statements from various fields will serve to illustrate this convenient form:

## Diagnostic Statements

FROM A MEDICAL SOCIAL DEPARTMENT.—Elderly, single, psychotic woman with slight cardiac limitation, who for many years has lived in self-imposed isolation on limited means. She is absorbed in a cause which she feels demands long, irregular hours of labor without compensation. Her refusal to regulate her life as to food and rest and her

[2] See next chapter.

overemphasis on her illness and discomfort are an outgrowth of her need for personal sacrifice and attention.

FROM A FAMILY AGENCY (PUBLIC).—Case of an American family consisting of a man, 35; his wife, 30; and three school-age boys. The family life is being undermined by drinking habits of the man, with a lowering of standards and undernourishment of the children ensuing. In addition to the problems of insufficient income, the oldest boy especially is suffering from being identified with his father, is sullen, unresponsive, and has recently joined an extremely undesirable gang where drinking is the main amusement.

FROM A FAMILY AGENCY (PUBLIC) FOLLOWING ELIGIBILITY STUDY.— Case of a widow, with two school-age children and one working, whose capacity to earn as a schoolteacher has been impaired by severe and protracted illness (nephritis). As she has no savings or other resources save the small earnings of the daughter, a condition of inadequate income and financial strain exist together with such marked tension and anxiety as to increase the disability and retard recovery.

FROM A FAMILY AGENCY (PRIVATE).—This is the case of a young adolescent girl with weak ego organization, who is so insecure and dependent that she is unable to participate in any group relations outside her immediate family. An unwanted and overprotected child with traumatic losses of first one parent and then another at critical ages, she brings to the problems of growing up great feelings of inadequacy and anxiety underlying her poor capacity for relationships. She is using her obesity (refusing to follow her diet and medical program)[3] as a defense against doing what the other girls do in sports, recreation, dances, especially since it protects her from meeting boys of whose attentions she is very much afraid.

FROM A FAMILY AGENCY (PRIVATE).—Miss L. is a 33-year-old Italian, Catholic unmarried mother, whose father is Greek Orthodox. She is in conflict with old world cultural and religious patterns and about keeping or placing her baby. Her guilt feeling is aggravated by a mother and siblings who feel that she has disgraced them. As the only child left with the mother, she assumes complete support for her, with elements of a self-imposed martyrdom and restitution. Her inability to make friends or relate very positively to people is an outcome of her great dependence on her mother. Her inability to give her baby up

[3]Note the parenthetical use of findings. After workers have learned to draw diagnostic conclusions they may introduce findings in dependent clauses to give more specificity to the interpretation

completely, although she cannot make plans for keeping him is also an expression of her feeling toward the baby's father, who refuses to marry her.

FROM A FAMILY AGENCY (PRIVATE).—Mrs. B., who is basically insecure in every type of human relationship, has functioned best when separated from her husband and children. She is unable to adjust in her marital relationship because of previous sexual experiences. Her anxiety about this is increased by her husband's need to keep her feeling inferior by constantly stressing her poor social background, inadequate schooling, and personal failures. Despite his criticism of her, she has been unwilling to effect a complete separation from him, saying she is sorry for him. She worries about her inability to make friends yet is unable to meet people halfway. She protects herself by an abusive, attacking manner, but is quick to take offense herself. She is insecure in her functioning as a mother, and expresses this through constant criticism of the children's care since their placement. She expects her son to assume a parental role toward the baby and has little conception of his own needs as a child, and is rejecting of the boy because of her feelings at the time of his conception.

She compensates for poor personal relationships by an excellent work record so far as production is concerned. She has some insight into her problems, is anxious for help and has been asking about psychiatric care.

The last paragraph has prognostic values.

FROM A CHILD GUIDANCE AGENCY (PUBLIC).—Jay's major difficulty centers around his refusal to attend school. Before leaving for school in the mornings he throws up, complains of aches and pains which have no organic basis, but over the week end he is all right. The onset of the present difficulty occurred when Jay was five and a half and in kindergarten. At that time his younger brother was born, and Jay refused to go back to school. Mother removed him at this time, but shortly afterward sent him to camp for the summer. In the fall she again had difficulty sending him to school. There seems to be strong sibling rivalry and resentment on Jay's part at being displaced at home by the younger brother. The mother handled preparation of the baby badly and did not make Jay feel wanted when the baby arrived.

The difficulty is one of long standing, the causes of which are inherent in the relationship of mother and child from infancy onwards. Mrs. S. was extremely disappointed at having a boy child. Her rejection of him is apparent in the harsh and punitive manner in which she handled him. There was little patience or toleration for him and an unbending, rigid program was outlined for him from birth. At a very early age the child was already showing signs of anxiety and insecurity, had all kinds of fears, was masturbating and reacting to certain situations by falling ill. The latter symptom has by now become an established pattern and is used in several ways by Jay, to avoid unpleasant situations and to attract the attention of the mother who, overcome by guilt during these times, indulges the boy to an excessive degree. Jay's falling ill also creates disharmony between the parents, since the father usually blames the mother for this. Jay appears to be aware of this and it may be his way of releasing some of the hostility he has for his mother.

The father is a nervous, withdrawn person, who is quite inconsistent in his handling of the boy. He, too, seeks an escape in illness. The mother reveals strong feelings of dislike for boys and this has undoubtedly contributed to the unsatisfactory marital relationship. With the father apparently quite inadequate, the mother is thus left with the disciplining of the children. However, because of her own lack of security, she seizes upon any method suggested to her and carries it out blindly.

FROM CHILDREN'S COURT.—Marie is an 11½-year-old girl, physically overdeveloped, immature, whose early experiences of rejection and neglect, as well as a continuing unstable family situation, manifest themselves in truancy and sex delinquency. Her insecurity with adults has made it necessary for her to test again and again whether she is really liked. The need for acceptance has continually manifested itself in her verbalizing, on a phantasy level, about the large allowances she receives and the many clothes she has—her criteria of what is desirable being clothes and money. Her bad and neglected health condition, in the form of enlarged and diseased tonsils and adenoids, as well as poor eyesight, further handicap Marie, causing retardation in her school adjustment, and postponing the planning for her of any healthier leisure-time activities. Marie is further confused by divided loyalties between her mother, her aunt, with whom she lives, her father, and her stepfather, all of whom tend largely to shift responsibility for her onto first one and then another.

In the foregoing diagnostic statements, and other similar ones, the paragraph on interpretation is usually followed by another paragraph showing plan of treatment, treatment goal (with or without prognosis) or some such content. Agencies show considerable variation at this point. Some do and some do not like the formal statement of treatment goal. The writer believes, however, that some indication of direction of treatment helps the worker in his thinking. Plan of treatment and prognosis, even though closely related to and usually following the diagnostic paragraph, is not the same thing as diagnosis in its narrower sense.

### Worker's Impression or Comment

Informal comments, though valuable, should not relieve us of the responsibility of a diagnostic statement giving the meaning of the case as a whole. Running comment within a recorded interview may be either of a diagnostic or evaluative type. As a by-product of process recording, one sees these partial comments usually related to some change in direction. Informal diagnostic writing can be very useful, although it is not in itself a substitute for the attempt to give the meaning of the case as a whole. Workers sometimes add a few lines at the beginning or end of an interview under the caption *Impression*. Comment of this sort should be related to what transpired in this particular interview. Diagnostic statements of the case as a whole should always be set off in separate paragraphs.

Diagnostic conferences are usually also informally written, although some follow agency patterns in presentation of case history, diagnostic summing up, planning for and evaluation of treatment. The styles used are of such mixed types that illustration is impracticable.

In the completest sense of process—reproducing the whole interview—comment by the worker would be included: "He said. . .," "I said. . .," "*I thought*. . . ." Here, the "I thought" is like the aside used on the stage. Trivial comments by the worker would have no place. If something the client says fits in as a new diagnostic piece in the worker's mind, this may be reflected by the parenthetical "I thought." Or, if something unusual is said by the worker because he is playing a diagnostic hunch, this may be explained in a comment.[4]

[4] It is sometimes used as a criticism of one's own technical handling.

Nine-year-old Bessie, whom I was seeing for the first time, came up to me and said, "Have you a daughter?" I replied, "no." She at once turned to the playthings and began a quite violent scene with the dolls. I realized that this was a mistake. The child was, in fact, reaching out for a mother, and this was a rejection to her.

Workers should be cautioned that a little of this goes a long way. Just as process itself should be used only for important interviews, so comment should be sparingly introduced within the text of the interview, and only for something which is not otherwise obvious.

### · MISCONCEPTIONS ABOUT DIAGNOSIS

Aside from the common mistake of confusing the evaluation and diagnostic processes, there are several other misconceptions. One concerns the purpose of diagnosis. Diagnosis is never made for its own sake; it is always made to help the client solve his problem; diagnosis is always for the purpose of treatment[5] Treatment itself in social case work runs along a scale from simple enabling help, through educational methods, to "therapy," and diagnosis becomes more and more important as we move from the case of the self-directing person with an "external" problem which he can see quite readily for himself to more complicated personality involvements. A recent paper refers to diagnosis as a "secret labelling of the client." [6] This is misleading. Here is no place to argue the merits of the question as to *whether* one should diagnose or not. This chapter explains for those who think diagnosis important, what it is and in what ways it may be recorded. The extent to which a client understands his own problem varies. Sometimes he understands it very

[5]Mary E. Richmond, *Social Diagnosis*, gave a brilliant analysis of social investigation, but the book as a whole emphasized the processes leading to diagnosis rather than diagnosis itself. "Social diagnosis (p. 357) may be described as the attempt to make as exact a definition as possible of the situation and personality of a human being in some social need—of his situation and personality, that is, in relation to the other human beings upon whom he in any way depends or who depend upon him, and in relation also to the social institutions of his community . . . the diagnostician, *who must have had social treatment in view from the very beginning*, has been measuring at every stage of his work the treatment value of each circumstance, each human relation and each personal characteristic."

[6]Jessie Taft, *A Functional Approach to Family Case Work*, p. 8

well indeed. Sometimes he sees only one aspect of it. He may or may not want to see any more  In many cases he does not see, face, or understand his own involvement in it. To work for insight may or may not be a realistic goal. It is true the case worker doesn't always understand the problem, but it is not quite true that "only as the client knows can I begin to know."[7] The worker must begin to know as best he can and as soon as possible. How deeply the diagnosis may be shared, or with what timing the meanings of a situation are apperceived and assimilated by the client is another question. In the "functional" approach the term "diagnosis" is used in an entirely different context, being regarded as "a developing process worked out by the client himself as he uses the agency service."[8]

Perhaps the most confusing aspect derives from the fact that we must reckon diagnostically with the person who has the problem. In the evolution of case work, objective problems were named first, and we had a stage in which classified problems stalked about, in a sense, with no owners. When at the height of the "passivity" period, relationships and attitudes towards problems were stressed, detached relationships and emotional abstractions flitted through the record pages like ghosts. Now we know that diagnosis should be anchored in a real social problem, but also we must show how the person is affected by his problem or involved in his problem. Actually in diagnosis we should always ask ourselves what is the problem; what pertinent causal factors may be discerned; how has the person been reacting to his problem; is the problem to be explained more or less by external or by internal factors, and the answers become our recorded diagnostic statement. In its fullest sense the statement must reckon also with the client's capacities and strengths, but usually in a paragraph showing prognosis or outlook for treatment.

Again, there is confusion between the method of arriving at diagnosis and the product itself. Social case workers used to derive diagnosis largely from social study or from social history;

[7]Helen Baum Lewis, "Case Work Notebook," *Social Work Today*, April, 1941, p. 17.
[8]K. L. M. Pray, *The Social Service Review*, June, 1945, p. 248.

now they also derive it from what takes place between worker and client in the interview, that is, through relationship. The historical facts are not in themselves diagnosis, nor are the "changing projections and identifications of the client" in the interview diagnosis. Findings are not the same as diagnosis. Diagnosis elicits the meaning of all the known and observed data. A child observed at play may recreate before our eyes his fantasy as to what is the matter at home, or we may learn about his problem from his parents and his school. The way a client uses his relationship with us informs us as to his relationships with others. But *however* we come to know, if and as we do come to know, let us write our interpretation carefully into the record as diagnosis.

Still another confusion arises from the fact that because a case moves, therefore the diagnosis must be said to change. A primary behavior problem in a child may turn into a character disorder in the adult; an unemployed person becomes partially employed, and so on. While this is true, it need not disturb us too much. To say diagnosis is tentative is not quite the same as to say it is always changing. Life is in constant flux, but diagnosis is a practical blueprint for a given purpose. A man turns up at a Red Cross desk. Diagnostically speaking, though on a descriptive level, he is AWOL, recovering from a hangover precipitated by anxiety about sailing and resulting in a lack of funds. You may say that when you have helped him recover himself, given him the necessary funds and other help toward turning himself in to the proper authorities, that the diagnosis has "changed." But most case workers would properly say that the immediate problem has been treated and, superficially at least, solved. The best advice is that whenever the diagnosis has substantially changed, or whenever it is proved wrong, let us make a fresh one. Otherwise we assume that it holds for the period of treatment.

### • SUMMARY

The diagnostic process attempts to answer the question "what is the matter." It is a professional opinion and should not be confused with the client's own statement of his problem which may or may not coincide with the professional formulation. Diagnosis is descriptive, defining, and it inherently strives to express causality. Although the diagnostic habit is more important than any form it may take, acceptance of the responsibility to formulate a diagnosis tends to improve skill in helping the client. Problem classification, diagnostic summary, diagnostic statement, and informal diagnostic writing, all have their place, the last two being the convenient forms for heavy case loads. The fact that diagnosis is always a tentative hypothesis, subject to revision, does not mean that it is in constant flux and so only to be expressed in running comment. Diagnosis should be made as early as possible, preferably within the first three or four contacts and thereafter reaffirmed, deepened or changed, as necessary. The diagnostic and evaluation processes are complementary though not identical, and a complete interpretation will demand both ways of eliciting the full meaning of a case. Since to grasp the dynamics of the case one must assess the client's capacities, his strengths as well as his weaknesses, and the balance of the whole picture, we must turn to a discussion of evaluation in the next chapter.

# 7

# UNDERSTANDING MUST INCLUDE
# APPRAISING SOCIAL VALUES

THAT THE PROCESSES OF DIAGNOSIS AND EVALUATION are related and interdependent does not mean that they are identical disciplines.

## · TOWARD WHAT ENDS DO WE WORK

Diagnosis, as we have shown in the last chapter, is concerned with understanding the nature of the difficulty presented to us; evaluation is concerned with ends in view, with social values and estimations. Change for the better, not change at random, nor regression, is the aim of treatment (or the helping process). Evaluation is always in terms of something: Is he strong enough? Strong enough for what? For manual labor, to recover, to work on his problem, or whatever. Workers usually find the process of evaluation easier to master than the process of diagnosis. It seems easier to estimate how well a person is managing his problem than to say what the problem precisely is. Some writers seem to minimize the diagnostic discipline,[1] and instead emphasize the evaluation process, the confusion perhaps arising from the use of an already established word in a new sense. In this approach the stress falls on the client's capacity to use services, or change, rather than on the nature of the problem and its

[1]Jessie Taft, in *A Functional Approach to Family Case Work* p. 8: "The functionally trained worker . . does expect to follow every client through the conflict which he experiences in trying to use help    The functional approach demands of the worker a fundamental understanding of change and growth, a deep comprehension of what it means to take help.    *The diagnosis is made* when worker and client arrive at a plan for continuing or finally terminating the contact." Also Almena Dawley, in *The Journal of Social Work Process* (1937), p. 27: "In this approach to understanding or diagnosis, whatever we may call it, we may *determine* to a degree the *client's readiness to do anything about his situation.*" (Italics the writer's.)

causes. Understanding both the nature of the problem and the client's readiness or capacity to work on his problem are, however, equally important. The process of evaluation of client strength is indispensable, but not as a substitute for diagnosis; and the writer believes the use of both terms is clearer than the use of either diagnosis or evaluation as the over-all word.

Early case records did not show always a distinction between fact and judgment, and still less between diagnostic and evaluative judgments. "She is quick and clever with her needle. . . . There is material for a good woman in her"; "She always has sound judgment and the gift of seeing through shams" (1906). "Blanche cried very pitifully, but tears are like April showers; can laugh or cry with ease but still seems to try to do what is asked of her" (1902). "Is very untruthful, but is capable—lovely with children and when she is good is very helpful, but the black moods come pretty often and then she is very ugly and is just as ungrateful as can be" (1904). "Family very intelligent, very funny; mother still crippled with rheumatism but does not now use crutches" (1908). "The house fairly clean, but Mrs. O. was untidy; plain to be seen that she is a drinking woman" (1912).[2] Such comments seem to us today subjective and naïve, but actually we cannot escape from concepts of positive and negative, normal and abnormal,[3] constructive and destructive strength and weakness, which is to say, we cannot escape from social values.

Basic to all practice in social work must be a conception of desirable and undesirable ends, goals, or outcome. To what extent a physical science can rid itself of the problem of values is often debated, but the essence of a social science lies not in mere accumulation of social facts, not in experience for the sake of experience, not in change for the sake of change, but in the moral purposes of civilization. Social work, even more explicitly, is directed not only towards material interests, full employment,

[2] "Case History Series," *Charity Organization Society Bulletin,* 1911
[3] LeRoy Maeder, "Diagnostic Criteria; the Concept of Norma and Abnormal," *The Family,* October, 1941. "Successful case work treatment involves a process of transition from the socially dislocated and deviant position of the client back to the usual position of equilibrium for that person." (Or, with new potentials for growth.)

adequate standard of living, but to ethical and aesthetic problems of society. Social work is concerned with self-determination,
with personal development with rights, with justice, with racial
and religious tolerance, with family security, with, in short,
democratic ideals. Professor MacIver goes so far as to say, "without goals or motives there are no social phenomena."[4] Social
work has nothing if it has not as its motivation the spirit of hu-
manity, which must comprise the whole texture of material
needs, moral rights, and social responsibilities. Treatment always contemplates alternatives, and these alternatives are
weighted for us in our culture. It is not only desirable to be a
socially adjusted or socially creative person, but this has new
potential values in itself. Even workers who seem to say, "We
have no goal but change, no end in view but movement or
change in some direction," do not really mean this, or they
would not be in social work. Early progressive education, which
showed the same fallacy of "self-expression for self-expression's
sake," has now regained its balance between experience and
purpose, between growth and knowledge.

When value judgments are projected ahead (Will the client
get better? Does he want to get better? Has he the capacity for
trying to get better, or for changing his situation? or what not?),
we call this process "prognosis." Whenever we look back over a
period of treatment or helping, we do so to appraise: How well
has the client been getting along? how well has our treatment
worked? How much improvement does he show? Has he been
able to hold his own? These are value, not diagnostic, judgments
and they occur in treatment evaluation. Whenever we look at a
foster home and study its strengths and weaknesses in terms of
its possible use for a child, we are again thinking in value terms.
One does not say, Is this a good home for a week-end party,
or for an architectural exhibit at the World's Fair? One must
ask in placement, Is this a good home for a child to grow up in?
Does it offer love, security, nutrition, as over against rigidity,
austerity, and deprivation (social value judgments)?

From the moment of application, therefore, the case worker

[4] R. M. MacIver, *Social Causation*, p. 271.

is not only trying to understand the problem-person configuration in diagnosis, but he is also trying to understand the person's capacity for using help, for helping himself, for movement, change, growth. If diagnosis is a sort of scientific understanding of the problem, evaluation is philosophical or ethical understanding of the purpose. We diagnose in order to be certain *what* it is we are asked to treat; we evaluate in order to discover how well the person is equipped for his journey, and whether it is a useful one. Mary Richmond saw the differences between diagnosis and evaluation and their interrelationship clearly.[5] She urged social workers to give the definition of the difficulty and the causal factors (diagnosis), and the *assets and liabilities*. What was this additional concept of hers—assets and liabilities? If a displaced person applies for resettlement, one weighs assets and liabilities. Will the kind of skill he brings be useful in community X? Has he the sort of wife who will help him make new contacts, or will she hinder him? Are they so dependent on their friends that they will be homesick and, therefore, a poor risk'? Evaluation, as already stated, balances positive against negative factors in arriving at a judgment.

### · TYPES OF EVALUATION

The common forms of evaluation include prognosis, often stated as a part of the treatment plan; treatment evaluation, and running comment related to a specific interview. Evaluation comes so naturally to us that we are hardly conscious of doing it, and much of it is informally expressed in records. Evaluation of a foster home, either in prospect or retrospect, has a distinctive function in child placing agencies. Other evaluations of social resources to be used in treatment are less fully recorded.[6] In diagnostic summaries evaluation is usually to be seen under such headings as treatment goal, and treatability or prognosis and as such should be accorded a separate paragraph which follows the diagnostic paragraph.

### Prognosis

Prognosis is usually found combined with plan of treatment: Fred needs psychiatric treatment, but at present this seems un-

[5]Mary E. Richmond, *Social Diagnosis.*    [6]See pp. 104.

feasible in view of the familial situation, which provides constant stimulus to anxiety. Mrs. Febel's immaturity and self-absorption make progress with her seem doubtful. It was agreed, however, to test further her capacity to relate herself to either Fred's problem or her own marital problem in terms of change. An after-school program—any group where Fred might find support and acceptance in the leader and where he'd have some opportunity for achievement, would be helpful.

. . . . .

In view of the resistance on the part of the parents and girl, it will be necessary to proceed slowly with Effie. In our brief contact Effie has blossomed out in response to an accepting attitude on the part of the worker. A treatment relationship can certainly be built up with this girl, which may be used to encourage her to grow up. With emotional support and opportunities for accomplishments in her chosen career, the mother may gain sufficient satisfactions to become less involved with the daughter.

As part of a diagnostic statement:

The combination of financial strain and chronic indebtedness now looks very difficult of solution. Despite the fact of good job and income, money, charged with all the dependency of the husband and the nagging demands of the wife, substitutes for the mutual affection they both crave. Their attractive social personalities and their many friends tend to block any real efforts at solution, since they are able to discharge their chronic irritability and tension by spending money on parties and liquor instead of saving for taxes, dentist bills and other unpleasant realities. Their desire for help is always translated into a request for someone to pay their debts.

The writer's suggestion that in recording diagnoses we distinguish (in separate paragraphs): a) the problems and the person's reaction to and involvement in his own problems, from b), the person's capacity to solve his problems with or without social case work help—is in the interest of simplifying and clarifying a very difficult kind of interpretation.

In the diagnostic summary used in one Child Guidance agency the headings are: statement of problem (reason for referral); development of present problem; significant factors in developmental history; emotional relationships; diagnostic statement (a paragraph which concludes with formal classification); therapeutic goal. Under the last we may read:

The objective in this case is to help Jimmy gain self-confidence, to become more independent, in which his superior intelligence, good health and musical talents should assist; to be relieved of his "bad moods" and use his abilities in a more constructive way with his school companions. The difficulty, however, is that Jimmy's problems are so interrelated with his mother's severe neurotic anxieties, that little may be accomplished if she proves inaccessible. Jimmy is so suspicious and shy that he will come slowly to have confidence in the worker. Jimmy's father, who has been rigid, punishing, and controlling, seems aware of his part in the problem, although his attempt to find answers in the psychological books may contain more resistance than he expresses. . . .

In the above, note the asset and liability or balancing construction, which is the characteristic movement in evaluation, whether fully expressed or merely implied.

A diagnostic statement from a medical social setting, with prognosis (evaluation).

Patient is an eleven-year-old girl who has had two seizures [idiopathic grand mal epilepsy], both occurring within the past two years and both so severe that hospitalization was necessary. Under medication she has had no attacks. Patient is using her illness to gain her own ends, particularly to get attention from her mother. She is stubborn, is fearful of new situations, and has food fads and a great craving for sweets. The older of two children—the other, a boy two years her junior, considered by parents a much easier child to handle, is all part of the picture of sibling rivalry. The parents are childish people who have a strong neurotic tie. Their ambivalence is marked, and they are now using patient's illness to punish each other. Father is an alcoholic and, though a person of considerable ability, has been a poor provider for his family. Financial insecurity and many moves have been added stresses in the family situation. Though fond of his children, father is lacking in any real sense of responsibility for them. Mother, who married her husband expecting to reform him, derives satisfaction alternately from mothering him and from playing the role of the martyr wife. She needs to stress her adequacy as a wife and mother, and his inadequacies as husband and father. She has always favored her son, and because of her guilt feelings has overprotected patient. This has been particularly marked since the onset of patient's illness.

Because of her good intelligence, success in school, and good relationship with other children, there are potentialities for patient's development and social adjustment. The prognosis for any basic change in the parents is poor because of their marked immaturity. Treatment in the area of their handling of patient and re-education of their attitudes toward her illness would seem to offer the best possibility, because mother recognizes that patient is using her illness and has asked for help.

## Treatment Evaluation

Originally the only treatment evaluation to be found in records was in the closing entry. In difficult or interesting cases or in cases carried for a long time, workers now analyze and evaluate treatment earlier than at the closing entry. Treatment evaluation summaries go beyond the point of appraising the results of treatment, to a discussion of the minutiae of technique, weighing successful as well as unsuccessful steps and attempting to account for relative improvement or lack of improvement. A treatment evaluation summary reviews progress in terms of the attempted solution or of growth, change, or movement, and usually concludes with a fresh plan or focus or renewed attempts along the lines of an old plan. A periodic summary bears the same relation to a treatment evaluation summary that a social study does to a diagnostic summary. A period summarized *in lieu* of chronological entries will have more factual data than a treatment evaluation made *in addition* to chronological entries. In other words, we always need a certain amount of evidence in the record. If the evidence is already there in successive entries, the worker can move directly into evaluation; if the evidence is not recorded, the treatment evaluation summary will give more detail.

From a family agency, a periodic summary April to July, *in lieu* of chronological entries:

Mrs. E. continued to move ahead during this period toward the attainment of the objectives she had set for herself. The thing she found most difficult to cope with was completion of her dental work, as it was necessary for her to go to the dental clinic two or three times a week during April and May. In addition, she found the treatments very painful, and was considered a difficult patient by the dental clinic as the doctors could not work on her mouth without giving her novocaine injections. Despite all her complaints of hardships involved for her in connection with this work, she was able to complete the major part of the work, and as a result of this experience, gained a further feeling of accomplishment in addition to relief of the pain from which she had been suffering. The total cost of the dental work done came to $43.25. Mrs. E. also undertook, during this period, activity in connection with the application to the Board of Child Welfare. The first step in this direction involved going to the National Desertion Bureau, which she did on 4/16. I gave her recognition for this step as another accomplishment, and she felt that it had not been hard for her as she knew it was something she had to do if she wanted help from the Board of Child Welfare. I recalled to her that when I first knew her she had wanted help from the Department of Welfare, and then from this agency, but had not found it as easy then to meet the requirements which were necessary to get that help. She recalled that at the time she had seriously considered committing suicide rather than going through all the investigations demanded of her. Everyone seemed to want to make things more difficult for her. Now people seem different to her. I said that actually the people were the same but perhaps she was different. She smilingly said that now she seems to look at the world through rose-colored glasses. There were times when it was not so rosy, but she was able to "take those times" differently than she had before. It did not make her feel as angry. . . .

She manifested some hostility in her complaints about the length of time it took before her application was acted upon, the numerous interviews she had to arrange for, and the fact that the investigator did not always keep her promise when she made any arrangements with her, but on the whole she was apparently able to deal with the situation in an entirely different way than when she first came to the agency and, as a matter of fact, the intake investigator who handled the situation at the Board of Child Welfare described Mrs. E. as "very cooperative."

The next evaluation from the same case shows a later and more concentrated interpretation.

During the past months Mrs. E. has gained a great deal of satisfaction from the things that she has been able to accomplish. She has traveled a long way from the time she tore up her Department of Welfare application because of her extreme resistance even to giving identifying information about herself to the present when she is able to deal with the Board of Child Welfare in a way that is described by them as "very cooperative." Apparently there has been a real change in her feeling toward people, which I felt from the beginning was her real problem.

Her feeling toward me has changed gradually from profound hostility and distrust to a beginning acceptance of me, and now, to complete confidence and trust in me. Also, during these past months this confidence has spread to include others. At first, as with the visiting nurse, she had to test her out considerably before trusting her, but gradually, as with the doctor, the dentist, and the investigator, Mrs. E. has begun to believe in people and to trust them to a degree. . . .

Since the time of the last evaluation Mrs. E. has consolidated the gains she made at that time as far as the child and her sister are concerned. She has drawn much closer to both of them and derives satisfaction from these relationships. As far as the baby is concerned, she has assumed complete responsibility for her care and for planning for her. As for her sister, I think that the feeling she has for her is something entirely new and related to the present. What has gone before, both in her relationship to her sister and to others, is still relatively unknown. Just as at first she seemed to reject the baby as the bad part of her, now her past seems to represent that and she still wants to push it away from her and from me.

At present her feeling is that I have contributed a great deal to the change in her and in her situation, but she feels strong enough within herself now to go on without me.

An excerpt from a treatment evaluation involving a large family:

The treatment was directed toward having each member take some responsibility for fixing up the home, having some regularity in their home management, in providing more adequate and physical supervisory care for Benito. The other members of the family were also interviewed around their interests, feelings, plans, and worker attempted some understanding and help with each one. The total family setting improved, each taking more interest and responsibility.

The intent of the interviews with Benito was to offer some interest, direction, and inject some notions of social behavior. He responded to the additional care he received at home and at school, plus the regular contact with worker. His truanting discontinued. He seemed happier, more active in clubs, and pleased with the extra things his father did for him, such as taking him out, etc.

The mother returned home and the family settled to a rather more regular way of life. She was able to contribute to the housekeeping and cooking, etc., and general standards improved. The housekeeping was immaculate and the place was more homelike. In November the family became upset as Elena had a psychotic episode. [See diagnosis: Dr. L. and hospital]. It seemed at first that commitment might be indicated, but within a few weeks she became more rational and seemed able to function somewhat. The psychiatrist's recommendation for treatment was to have her parents give her as much attention as possible and to develop the relationship with worker and encourage her normal activities. She has responded to this and is now employed and has some social outlets. . . . . .

Evaluation used early in a case:

At the time of the above interview we had been helping Mrs. R. financially for a month with the understanding that it was on a short-time basis, and to enable her to work out plans for herself. Mrs. R. talked about getting a job the first week we helped her and from then on, but never seemed to do anything about it. During the first two weeks of our help her husband was still at home, and she claimed she had to take care of him. After he was admitted to the institution she found other excuses and said she was busy attending to various matters such as the union, the compensation case, etc.

We felt that Mrs. R. still wanted to remain a dependent, infantile person and was afraid to meet the responsibility suddenly thrust on her shoulders. She wanted us to go on helping her from week to week until her husband was well again. When she became less certain of our continuing help she began to consider the possibility of taking a job more seriously. She seemed to have very ambivalent feelings about taking a job. On the one hand she was very scared of this idea as it would mean definitely taking on responsibility, doing something she had never done before, and dealing as an adult with a cold business world where she might easily be hurt. On the other hand she was afraid that we might stop helping her before Mr. R. was able to go back to work, and she seemed to dread the idea of going to public assistance.

Whenever she did consider a job, she thought of a temporary or part-time one, as she hoped her husband would be well enough to work soon, and thus relieve her of this burden.

We were convinced that Mrs. R. would not move in any direction as long as we continued to help her from week to week without setting up any limits. She seemed to be trying to use us in much the same way as she had used her mother and then her husband. In this interview I used agency limitations to force Mrs. R. into making a choice and decide on some plan of action. She could either decide to try with us or to get help of relatives and friends. However, any of these choices meant that she could no longer just dump all her problems on the agency and have us take care of her. We felt that if Mrs. R. did decide to get a job and succeeded in this that she would become a much more mature, and more self-sufficient person, and would no longer feel as hopeless in a hostile world. However, such a decision would really have to be hers. That is why I tried to draw out her ambivalent feelings about taking a job and tried to help her to know if this was really what she wanted to do.

*Evaluation in the use of a temporary foster home.* The summary covers a three month's period during which regular visits were made, and is in lieu of chronological entries:

Joan has made remarkable progress in the home although she is still a difficult baby with regard to eating. When she was first placed she looked like a pale and haggard old woman, and in these few months she has changed considerably even in physical appearance. She is alert and fairly active; she raises herself but not yet to a sitting position, although she does sit nicely. Our doctor referred her in July for an examination for rickets. At the present time there is no doubt that she is in excellent health; her color has improved greatly and she has gained weight steadily. She is even pretty now in a piquant way. She sleeps well and has become on the whole a happier baby, but eating is still a problem for her. When vegetables were first introduced into her diet, she resisted them by developing almost a temper tantrum at feeding time.

Foster mother suffered a great deal of anxiety over this but I was able to help to relieve this so that we could work out experimenting a little with Joan. After her refusal to take any food for over twenty hours at one time, foster mother introduced vegetables and cereal in a bottle; every few days she would attempt to spoon-feed Joan, but each time the baby refused the spoon. Nevertheless, Joan has been eating well since that time.

Foster mother and the rest of the family have derived a great deal of pleasure from taking care of Joan, especially in watching the great progress she has made. Foster mother nevertheless continued to talk about the first two foster children she had. In discussing her difference of feeling toward Joan I recognized with her that she was deliberately trying to remain less attached to Joan; she enjoyed being a temporary foster mother and yet after two separations she felt that another would be difficult, especially if Joan were to remain as long as the other two children had. We discussed at one time the possibility of her taking two children from us when we had an emergency with which I hoped she could help us out. Foster mother feels that one child is just all she can ever care for because she does have a great deal of work with her own two children, and her husband's irregular hours of work also make this impossible.

Foster mother shared freely with me her feelings about the mother and the grandmother visiting in the home. At first she thought they were "nice people" and she was pleased with their regular visiting and their great interest in Joan. Later, as she became more attached to the baby, she was quite upset that they "only talked" about taking her home. I explored her feelings with her about taking care of someone else's child who is definitely not one's own and yet wanting at least that the parent do right by the child. Foster mother tended to give them advice and we talked about our mutual roles with regard to the mother. It was with great difficulty that she recognized with me that the agency wasn't here to reform every mother who places her child in a foster home, and that the most she can do is to give the parents an opportunity to know the child; and come to their own decision for the future through this experience. I felt her growing unwillingness to hold out with Joan until we can arrange for a long-time home.

### Another from the child placing field:[7]

This period has been a threatening and uncertain one for Mrs. T. Faced with a new worker to carry out the replacement of Johnny which she so strongly resisted, the foster mother's fear and active hostility toward the agency was dominant. The recent loss of her husband and the imminence of losing her son to the Army, as well as her emotional need to have a child dependent upon her, all made it im-

[7] For evaluation of a foster home, as such, see p. 106.

possible for Mrs. T. to help Johnny through this separation experience. The need for replacement had been put on the basis that she was now working, and also that we want a normal family structure—both foster parents—for our children. Our feeling that with only Mrs. T. in the home, the balance of negative and positive factors had been dangerously impaired, was not shared with the foster family.

Mrs. T.'s bitter struggle with us to keep Johnny, created in the child a deep sense of guilt and fear that he had irreparably injured the foster mother in having left her. Because of this, and also because of the satisfaction he had derived from her completely indulging and dependent love, the youngster was unable to tear himself out of his relationship and to form any meaningful attachments in another home. After 3 months of temporary placement, we decided to re-evaluate the situation in the T. home to see if Johnny might be returned.

Throughout this time, Mrs. T. repeatedly offered to give up work if she could get Johnny. Though Mrs. T. was more controlled than usual, she could not accept our sincerity in this desire to effect replacement of the youngster with her. There was a strong emotional factor in her need to maintain financial independence, and therefore to keep her job. She could not face dependence upon her stepsons. However, she expressed quite frankly that she had to test the agency further before she would put herself "at its mercy." This element was present in her refusal to move toward consideration of any other plan that would offer some degree of financial independence and still permit her to serve Johnny as a foster mother. Her need to have the child on her terms alone reflected, as well as indicated, a need to possess Johnny completely, and a total inability to share responsibility with an agency. It was made clear that it was Mrs. T. who was rejecting all ways of making it possible for Johnny to return. She accepted too that this decision had to be the final one.

### · SUMMARY

The diagnostic question, what is the matter and what was causal? and how is the person reacting to his problem? must always be accompanied by evaluation questions: toward what end is he striving? what strengths and capacities can he muster to solve his problem or to use the worker or the agency for his goals? Nor can we be indifferent to the nature of his goals. We cannot say it is nothing to us whether he gets better or worse, stays comfortable or uncomfortable, rejects his children, lives in squalor, is undernourished or unemployed or ill. It is true that we must not impose *our* plans or goals upon him, force him to our way of thinking about social values, but it is equally true that we cannot be neutral as to the outcome for him. Our skills are there to help the individual become what he and he alone is capable of becoming, but in terms of his well-faring, not ill-faring. The client must measure himself within a culture, within social reality. Evaluation looks forward in prognosis, which is usually associated in the record with treatment planning, or looks reflectively back on the success or failure of treatment in evaluation summaries. Some evaluation is almost always seen in closing entries. Diagnostic thinking is purely descriptive and etiological, without consideration of better or worse; evaluation, or weighing, always suggests a preferential course of action or goal, either in retrospect or prospect. Current practice tends to use the term diagnosis interchangeably with evaluation; the writer believes we gain in precision by the use of each term in a differentiated but complementary sense to cover the total understanding of a case.

# 8

## *AGENCY STRUCTURE, FUNCTION,*
## *AND POLICIES CONDITION RECORDING*

W<small>HILE THE BASIC PROCESSES IN RECORDING REMAIN</small>
essentially constant for all fields, agency purposes and program
determine contents and, to some degree, style in recording.
More differences will be found between agency and agency than
between field and field. There will always be more difference in
recording between professionally trained and untrained workers
than among the several fields, since whatever is not developed
within practice cannot be found in the reports of practice. Assuming mastery of the component processes—narrative and summary writing for the reporting of facts; diagnosis and evaluation
for the reporting of the worker's interpretation of the facts—
what may we emphasize in addition as characteristic of certain
fields? As it is not practicable to comment on all variations, the
records in public assistance, child placing, hospitals, institutions, and "short contact" agencies have been arbitrarily selected because of certain special problems in each of these large
fields.

· *PUBLIC ASSISTANCE*

Public welfare records are of the family agency type and follow the practices already described. It is important to remember
that just as in a medical-social record the medical features of
the case should be clearly denoted, so in any form of relief administration the economic-social data should be emphasized.
This is true whether in the United Nations Relief and Rehabili-
tation Administration or a security agency, or any voluntary
agency carrying major relief functions.

Since the central purpose of a public assistance program is to provide income to those eligible persons who are in need, economic or financial social data have a central place, but the recipient is a social being with all the associations, feelings, and personal reactions of other men. He may or may not have achieved a comfortable balance between internal pressures and external strains. He may or may not have family problems intimately bound up with the economic problem. His difficulties may or may not be resolved when he is provided with an income. He, like others, has claim to whatever goods and services his culture makes available to him.

This assumption implies acceptance of the applicant, respecting his rights, taking into consideration his attitudes, eliciting his participation, accrediting his strengths, encouraging his sense of responsibility, making available to him the resources of the agency and community appropriate to his welfare. Translated into skills, these case work operations become the proper business of the assistance agency and the proper contents of the record.

Because of the statutory basis of eligibility and the reimbursement of monies expended, social evidence must be fully and accurately recorded. The process of determining eligibility is itself of primary importance for the record. While the review of eligibility as required by law and regulation unfortunately conduces both to stereotyping and repetition, workers can guard against this tendency by thinking about the *person*. In a real situation which either changes or does not change for him, it is, of course, the changes, if any, which must be recorded. Any significant reactions to agency requirements on the part of the recipient, whether at intake or later, should always be noted. Workers are not always interested in or sufficiently careful about the recording and revision of budgets or financial discussions. The client's estimate of expenses and the discussion of it deserve a place. Unmet needs, even those not within the function of the agency, should be noted either because of possible referral or as a basis for long-range planning and social action.

Beyond these points, criticism of the commonest deficiencies

—which are not unique in any field—in public assistance records today would suggest: records are often so meager (from lack of information, not from proper condensation) that it is hard to know what has gone on; the client is not individualized; the main services of the agency are not clearly described; the worker's role in giving information or services is not indicated; there is little interpretive writing even on eligibility; the flow of the case—what happened—is not clear; children, even when the objects of the program, do not emerge except as items in the budget; and there is much irrelevant and subjective comment.

There is always a tendency to take too much of the worker's time and too much record space in bookkeeping. The fewer financial transactions of a "cashier" type in the record, the better. The case worker is responsible for describing the family finances and for estimating the family budget, for periodic comments on the rate and nature of the assistance, and particularly for noticing changes, but the actual posting of commodities, money payments, and so on, is an accounting job which should be dealt with through ledgers and other devices. Workers should know the rates in the assistance, may keep rough totals of the amount granted, may consult the ledger card from time to time, or better still may be furnished periodically by the accounting department with totals drawn from the ledger. These totals may then appear in the text, or in periodic summaries, with appropriate comment by the worker.

A question usually arises in connection with forms. Public records tend to the use of forms because of the necessity for standardization in accordance with governmental framework. Many agencies face the problem of duplicating forms, but the public agency is especially cumbered with overlapping data, among application blank, face sheet, budget and statistical cards. Confronted by this array, many workers try to evade the issue by carrying these data around with them in their field books. Workers should be trained to relinquish the bulk of financial, identifying, and permanent data to the proper record, and to use their books for notes on situations and behavior as a basis for the social contents of the record. They should also *read* the records more and thus avoid repetition.

It is important to have a simple face sheet, although the application blank may be a practical substitute. One of the best combinations is that of identifying material on the front of an 8 x 11 card with a budget on the back, ruled to permit revisions. This card belongs either in the case record or as a desk file in an alphabetized box for each worker. Obviously, since this card is and should be much used, it should be accessible at all times, both with and without the rest of the record. Face sheet material and detailed budget computation should not be repeated in the text, but changes in family status or of grant, or other pertinent comment, should appear in the text. If it is administratively necessary to copy face sheet material upon several cards, efficiency suggests that the arrangement and naming of the material on the forms be similar. It is difficult to copy an item in an upper left-hand box on one form and have the same item appear, with a slight variation, in a lower right-hand box on another form.

Some state auditors[1] have assumed that they may check the validity of the eligibility data through the case record. This would seem as inappropriate as auditing hospital finances on the medical chart to supervise admission of patients. The determination and review of eligibility is a welfare, not an auditing function. It is proper that summarized financial data reports, with or without budget compilation, should be made available to auditors, but the case record is a study and service document developed not for fiscal purposes, but for everyday use by the persons most concerned and therefore most competent to shape it to efficient welfare practice.

The exacting regulations governing eligibility in the field carry an administrative counterpart in the office. Appropriate and skilled case work operations are often found overlaid with inappropriate clerical duties, such as, the writing of vouchers, filing and tracing records, mailing checks, posting grants, typing, thus making the necessary eligibility, budgetary, and authorization procedures irksome and protracted. Financial data cards,

[1]The auditor referred to here is the financial auditor associated with the comptroller's function. "Case reviewers" or "social auditors," that is, case workers assigned to this task from the Welfare Department, are qualified by experience to read and evaluate eligibility data.

monthly reports, case load analyses, statistical counts, and authorization and reauthorization reports must be prepared as part of the administrative function, but not as part of the case record. It is the administrator's responsibility to see that statistical, accounting, and case procedures supplement and inform, but do not exploit, each other. In too many organizations the communications go from case to business departments without a corresponding service from business to case, and the statistical operations are all too frequently superimposed. The effect of interchange and joint planning is almost always a reduction and simplification of forms. When services, such as resource departments and nutrition departments, become isolated, they not only tend to function extravagantly, but usually, to everyone's inconvenience, give birth to quantities of forms and reports, and virtually to duplicate case records. Nevertheless, useful forms include budget, occupational, insurance adjustment, mortgage and property blanks, and medical data. Forms intended for the case record should be of approximately the same size and shape, but may be differentiated by color. Forms intended for the mechanics of administration may be of any shape suitable for filing.

If it is important to reduce the total number of forms in the record, it is equally so to reduce the number of successive copies of the same form. If a new application blank is filed, it is not necessary to retain the old one. Any discrepancy or change should be noted on the new blank and referred to in the text. The notion that restitution proceedings depend on the presence in the record of the original application blank seems to be neither true nor useful. Nor should old authorizations be retained. The date of approval of grant will appear on the financial- and social-data card. There is some reason to keep the last authorizations, temporarily, for the convenience of the social worker; but stacks of these, or of social service exchange clearing slips, or of work-referral duplicates, do no one any good.

As to the main style of the record, a combination of narrative and summary is usually the most effective. As in other fields, if personality factors, attitudes and behavior in the financial assistance area are conspicuous, narrative, with index headings to point up the eligibility features may be chosen, whereas, if the economic problem is uncomplicated, summary style may prove more convenient. In either event the study material, showing each factor of eligibility and what help the applicant is requesting, should be followed by a (diagnostic) statement of the economic social situation, that is, one which defines the problem and describes the eligibility status. Next, a recommendation as to the grant and other services, if indicated. Thereafter, most of the follow-up may be carried through periodic summaries, with occasional use of narrative for important interviews.

There are those who contend that in a public agency chronological entries are safer than summary, since in the event of mistakes or complaints or appeals or special investigations they afford greater protection to client, worker, and administrator. Supervisors with untrained staffs often encourage the chronological narrative entry so that they can see the course of investigation and service more easily; but it is certainly true that in competent hands selective summary, diagnostic thinking, and condensation of all kinds are not only economical but adequate.

It is not necessary to report the initial application interview verbatim or in full detail, but because it reveals the client's own sense of what is wrong, the story may well be given with selected use of the applicant's own phraseology, reflecting his own emotional stresses.[2] The public assistance record suffers from an excess of procedures as well as forms. Standardized procedures involving work referral or medical care, like those involving eligibility and authorization, call for accurate notation, but so far as possible, mechanics, as well as trivialities, should be avoided. A long list of phrases for omission might include:

Worker compiled a budget as follows.
Worker will notify Miss L. of the result of the interview.
Interview took about one-half hour.
Worker left interview to consult supervisor.

[2]This is consistent with Federal Security Agency, since the applicant is regarded as the primary source of information in determining eligibility.

A further report may be obtained after next Monday.
Two quarts of milk approved by supervisor.
Mr. D. then left the department, thanking worker for his time.
Took off wet coat at worker's suggestion.
Received and read case.
Sent new authorization to order-writing department.
Checked February payroll. All three names are included, but the address has not been changed.

Entries on the making of appointments, unless there is something significant about the circumstances, or behavior, should be omitted. Usually the redundancy occurs because the dictation period precedes the expected appointment, but the earlier steps may be solemnly dictated even though Mr. Jones may have come and gone as expected. Routine relief issuance, routine follow-up letters, and the ordinary courtesies of the ordinary interview, should also be omitted.

Agencies may fall into the bad habit of including in the transfer summary procedural directions for the next authorization, for example:

> Family moving out of district.
> Unit of 3—man, woman and 4-yr.-old son.
> Food allowance $10.60.
> Rent allowance $8.70.
> Gas and light allowance to be checked.
> SC–4 completed.
> Moving to new address, where light and gas allowance is needed 518 W. 213. Apt. 3C.

Rather, workers should be taught to consult the budget and find the new address on the face card.

Army and veterans' records conform to the family and public assistance type of record. Because of regulations, claims, and other standardized governmental procedures, forms are typical. Face sheets and application blanks always contain the essential army identifying data, and history outlines carry special headings such as "discharge status." Correspondence usually requires a client consent slip, which is more and more part of good practice in requesting reports for others than veterans. Correspondence which is apt to be voluminous is filed preferably in chronological sequence at the back of the folder, with appropriate notation in the text.

### · CHILD PLACING

In so far as a "children's" agency deals with children in their own homes, the record follows the pattern of the "family" agency. It is only when child placing is undertaken that special recording problems arise. Even so, because the psychological ties of parent and child or of siblings have become recognized, there is a tendency toward as integrated a case history as possible. Child placing always demands a specially accurate record of where the child is to be found, because of the quasi-parental responsibilities assumed by the agency. Face sheet information should be checked and revised whenever a significant change has occurred in the composition or status of the family group. Accuracy of addresses for child, parents, guardians, and foster parents is a first essential when the child is out of the home.

A child placing record reflects the parental situation which precipitates separation, preparation of parent, child, and foster parents for the separation experience;[3] with periodic evaluations of the child's growth and progress in foster care.

The children's field, like other fields, tended in the early days to a structuralized record with a topical social study, including medical and psychological summaries, before placing, but the subsequent entries were usually chronological. Because of intake practices which still obtain in family-children-and-court agencies in certain localities, it is not unusual to find a child

[3]See "Recording Child-Welfare Services," Bureau Publication No. 269. United States Department of Labor, Children's Bureau, 1941, p. 24 *et seq.* "The running record of treatment should contain statements regarding the arrangements that have been made with the parents, the foster parents, and the agency responsible for the child. It should also show the way in which the parents and the child met the separation and the way in which the child met the new experience, his acceptance by the foster family, and his response to them . The flow of the record should indicate whether the worker assumes major treatment of the child's problems or whether such treatment is being carried indirectly through the foster parents. The reasons for the plan of treatment should be clear as they relate to the purpose and length of placement, the relationship to the child that is maintained by the natural parents, and the foster parents' ability to understand the child and his family and to be of help to them," (p. 26).

placing record beginning with a summarized history from another agency or division. But the agencies which do a whole case work job, including intake, which think of the family as a unit and treat it in relation to the placed-out child or children, reveal this development in a more fluid record. The segmental approach, like the early departmentalized record of other agencies, seems to be passing, or at least to be greatly modified by integrative practices. One may still see an arrangement in which the family of origin has one folder, the foster family with placed-out children has a second folder, of the family agency type, and each child has in addition his own folder. The important thing is to keep the own family, foster family, and child interaction in the same case record if possible. With siblings placed in separate foster homes, it is usual to open a separate folder for each. If the children are reunited it is often possible to combine the folders or, after making a careful summary of the second child, close out this folder and continue as in a family record. The record, by indexing, headings, colored pages, and other devices, may bring out any child as "patient" within the family framework.

A characteristic of child placing is that separate records are necessary for the home-finding process, because the home is used for successive children or for several families at once. The selection of foster parents, through application and home study and the subsequent review and evaluation of the home, are kept in one folder. The strengths and weaknesses of the foster home are appraised much as those of the own home, with the stress falling on the warmth, maturity, and adequacy of the human beings who are to act as substitute parents. An additional feature is the appraisal of the foster parents' ability and willingness to meet the agency's requirements, and to work with it in a shared responsibility. Most agencies record the rejection of an applicant requesting to board children as carefully as the acceptance. This conforms to a somewhat general principle which also applies in public assistance, that reasons for rejection should be always clearly stated in case of appeal, reapplication, or community pressure.

As an example of rejection:

Mrs. W. in office. She was poised and extremely self-contained as she greeted me; as soon as we sat down she seemed almost literally to be holding herself together. She said immediately that she knew why I had asked her to come in. I recognized the great emotional strain she had been under when she saw Norman; she had had such a difficult time of it that I couldn't talk to her about it at that time and yet I thought that we would have to examine together just what had happened and how she felt about it in terms of our going ahead together. She began to tell me then, relaxing more and more as she talked, of how she couldn't look at a baby without thinking of her own, how she couldn't stand seeing diapers; she couldn't think of having someone dependent on her as a baby is; then she said almost hopelessly that perhaps she would just have to take a child who was a little older, who could walk and talk. I wondered whether this was what she really wanted. I knew that she had come to me saying that a child was what she really wanted to enrich her life. We had seen each other and had proceeded assuming that this was so, and now I was questioning that. I wondered whether she could bring herself to question this desire of hers also. Was I really knocking the ground out from under her? She said she did learn something from this experience, that she could tell me truthfully she doesn't want a baby because she would have to give so much to a small child. I felt she was telling me she had come to me because she wanted another satisfaction out of life and she thought a child would give that other satisfaction. Yes, she said, that was exactly it. That was why she saw now she wanted an older child, who could give it to her. I explored with her the question of how much of a difference there really would be with an older child. Sure, the diapers wouldn't be there, and the child could walk and talk by himself, but could we say a child of three or four is independent? At first she tried to argue with me around the details of care for an older child; then, she said this isn't what she wants. I could understand how painful it was for her to go away now without a child but, even more, without the solution she thought she had found. She said then, "No, you're wrong there. We haven't wasted our time together. I came here wanting a child and now I'm going away without one, that's true. But I'm also going away knowing that I don't want one. That's settled, and it's better that this didn't come out after the child was already in my home." I was glad we could say goodbye with that; we had been through a difficult experience together and I knew that Mrs. W. had come out all right. She thanked me for helping her and said, as she left, I had also helped her husband through her.

An evaluation of a foster home has a good deal of evidence in regard to its use for one or more children:[4]

Mrs. R., foster mother, makes an excellent first impression of warmth and motherliness. She continues to be friendly and at ease in her relations with the worker, but increasingly shows a rigid personality. She has rather old-fashioned ideas of child training and does not respond well to suggestions, particularly around Calvin's emotional needs. She is highly respected in her community (predominantly white) and is anxious to maintain this position. Because she feels that Calvin's mischief is a reflection on her ability, she tends to keep him around the home, thus exaggerating the sibling rivalry which exists between the two boys. Mrs. R. is accepting of Calvin although not of all his behavior. She is not sure whether she would want to accept other children with similar problems. While she has intellectual understanding of Calvin's difficulties, she is not able to use this in practice. She is inclined to think Calvin does not need as much affection as the other child because he has a mother.

Mrs. R. approves of a good child, and although she consciously tries to treat Calvin and his companion equally well, Calvin is often the one in disfavor. She is ashamed of his backwardness and is interested in helping him improve his schoolwork. She attributes his school failure to purely physical causes. It is significant that she could handle Calvin's stealing well, but not his sex play. She has considerable feeling around the sexual area and retreats from a recognition of it as a problem even though she knows it exists. Mrs. R. is occasionally discouraged and needs support and assurance that she is effecting improvement in Calvin. She gets satisfaction from the fact that as a foster mother she is giving a real service to the community. While she preferred not to have two workers, she has made the second one feel welcome and is increasingly able to separate Calvin's activities from those of the other child. She has a good understanding of the role of the worker and uses it well. Mrs. R. has assumed a motherly attitude toward Calvin's mother, and is protective of Calvin in discussions with her.

[4]See pp. 92–94 for further illustrations of foster-home evaluations.

Mrs. R.'s brother has assumed the role of foster father to a much greater degree than was expected. From Mrs. R.'s reports he seems to take an active interest in Calvin, is tolerant and kind, and is enjoying his fatherly role.

This home gives Calvin good physical care, but lacks understanding of his emotional needs. The rather rigid behavior requirements and sharp curtailment of play activities to a limited area has helped to keep Calvin tense, submissive, and secretive. His explosive behavior now tends to take place in the school.

Later periodic evaluations can be a good deal condensed since the primary evidence can always be looked up through cross-reference to a given child's record while under care. Recapitulation of factual detail should, as in all skilled evaluation, be reduced to a minimum.

Hospital, court, and institutional records share certain characteristics deriving from the fact that social service acts as part of a team. There is a general trend toward the use of a unit record,[5] and because of the orchestration the main and subsidiary functions have to be clearly worked out and economically recorded.

## · MEDICAL SOCIAL RECORDS

In medical social work, the unit record is contributed to by physicians, social workers, nurses, and technicians. Administrative details of finance and bills are usually kept in the superintendent's office or other appropriate place. Eligibility studies, which belong in the unit record, as a basis for free or low-rate care, are like any other economic-social study except as they are pointed up to the health needs of the patient. The meaning of the patient's illness to him as a unique person in his own peculiar situation should be clearly presented and the social material should be organized and arranged so that it will effectively point up its relation to medical-social diagnosis and treatment. Many social service departments keep the social chart separately, putting only summarized material in the medical record, but

[5]See p. 12. See also *Bulletin of the American Association of Medical Social Workers,* July, 1945, p. 46.

the trend which has been strongly moving toward better medical social integration finds its expression in a unit record. In the unit record colored sheets for social service functions are common, with additional notes which are made on the follow-up, or continuation sheets, which all professional services use. On the social service sheets, medical social interpretation of the problem will be found, and often instructions as to diet, who is to assume responsibility for certain treatments or precautions, specific instructions for plastic surgery cases, and so on.

A mechanical problem in all hospital recording is that the medical chart is about a single patient, whereas medical social work, like all case work, is interpersonal. The social history and follow-up notes are, therefore, placed on the "primary" patient's chart with summaries on the other members of the family who may be patients. Cross-reference is important. Summaries, if time permits, are better than carbons, which are usually not well enough focused to the special problem. Because the social area is so complex, workers using the unit medical record have to subject themselves to rigid disciplines of selection and condensation lest the social material overwhelm the medical. Many doctors, accustomed to medical abbreviations, will not take the time to examine long social work entries, and even if they would, the problem of bulk makes such documents questionable. Social entries should be relevant, non-technical, and concise, which is good advice for anyone.

Objections to the unit record include the danger that in large institutions the confidential nature of the record may not be guaranteed. Even if records are not subpoenaed, it is hard to protect intimate social material against casual examination. Moreover, unless record library facilities are extremely accessible and competently directed the unit chart may not be available to the several persons wanting simultaneous use of it. A few agencies with departmentalized structure—although this is not characteristic of medical work especially—prefer an "assembled" rather than a unit record. Departmental notes are clipped or bound together and inserted in a common folder or envelope to be withdrawn separately at will. While this makes for greater flexibility in handling, it defeats the unified purpose, since departments tend to draw out their own special material, and therefore this practice cannot be recommended.

The social service notes placed on follow-up sheets are designed to flag the physician's attention with an item which bears directly on the medical problem, for example, health and medical data which did not appear in the anamnesis; reports from private physicians and visiting nurses; work and diet and conditions at home which may be inducing anxiety or tension or upset. For convenience, these brief notes may be typed on a sticker and pasted on the page in chronological order between two notes by the physician. Two illustrations follow:

*1.4.36.*—On December 27th, 1935, letter received from patient stating he was entirely without funds. Patient referred to Seamen's House, where he was given $4.00 in cash and told to return there for a room and board if he desires. Doctor has advised against work at present because of the danger of infection to the wound, but patient is very restive about this. Further arrangements for financial assistance will be made. See social service history for occupational situation and problem.

. . . . .

*11.25.42.*—Patient's husband told social worker that patient was, for nearly a year in the State Hospital. Following report was secured: "Patient admitted July 1933, discharged March, 1934; paroled for one year and discharged as "recovered" in 1935. Diagnosis: Manic Depressive Attack, Depressed Type.

The following type of note would appear on the social service sheets rather than on the follow-up medical sheets, for obvious reasons. The details were given because of the danger of gangrene and the importance of close supervision.

*Discharge Plan*

*1.19.37.*—This patient is going home today with her daughter. Visiting nurse will see the patient once a week. The patient's foot is almost entirely healed and needs only a dry dressing. The daughter has been instructed that the patient's feet should be washed each day with warm soap and water, dried thoroughly and powdered. She should wear white cotton socks, clean each day, and over these warm woolen socks and soft bedroom slippers. She is being discharged on 20-0-20 insulin and her daughter has consulted the dietitian. The daughter is at home in the morning to give the patient the insulin and will measure the insulin, leaving the proper amount in the syringe so that the patient can give it to herself in the evening. (Patient's daughter away at work from noon until 10 p.m.) Patient will be alone from 4:30 until 10:00 except for the daughter's husband who cannot be counted on to supervise. We realize that this arrangement is not good and that patient should not be allowed to give herself her evening insulin, but it is the best arrangement that can be made at the moment. Patient has been given an appointment to go to Orthopedic Hospital for advice re: proper shoes, and daughter will see that the housekeeper takes her.

Because so much medical social treatment deals with sick people, for whom mobilizing of resources must be of an active, practical sort, or because treatment may consist of interpretation of the medical problem to patients and their families along familiar lines, process has until recently not been much featured. In many hospitals social case workers are not part of the admitting process, so that the fully recorded intake interview giving the patient's spontaneous story is not typical. In many hospitals also, size of case load and attitudes of medical staff toward emotional material have made the case workers center their attention, for the most part, on services of practical helpfulness, rather than on the subtler uses of case work relationship in the interview. As medicine, and consequently medical social work, has incorporated more of the psychosomatic and psychiatric emphases,[6] case records contain more processes geared to psychological reassurance, "supportive" treatment, and insight as well as guidance and interpretation. Workers operating at this level have to be so sure-footed that they can either use "process" when indicated or take a short cut through diagnostic and evaluation comment, as pointed out in earlier chapters. If separate rather than unit records are used these will conform to all the ordinary recording practices of a social agency as previously discussed.

[6]See Eleanor Cockerill, "Psychiatric Understanding with Surgical Patients." *The Family*, February, 1943. See also pp 63–87 for additional illustrations.

Medical social consultation in public welfare, work with crippled children, and similar programs usually follow the public assistance family type record.

### · PSYCHIATRIC AND CHILD GUIDANCE RECORDS

Distinctive differences between hospital records in psychiatric and medical social work have not emerged. The psychiatric hospital record often features a follow-up supervisory report on paroled patients which is formally, and sometimes too rigidly, geared to the psychiatrist's angle of interest. As in medical social work, all notes have to be concise and relevant. Emotional material naturally receives much attention, but full reporting of worker-patient relationships have often been minimized because of some of the institutional and team reasons already mentioned. The trend here also is, nevertheless, toward more fluidity in reporting the social work contribution to treatment.

Child guidance records by contrast are typically long contact, intensive records with a great deal of verbatim material. They are always of the team approach and unit character. At one time the fourfold study[7] routinely included the work-up of psychiatrist, physician, psychologist, and case worker. Today the combinations are selective, the timing of tests much more carefully prepared for and not always insisted upon. The parent-child relationship is always to be found in one folder. If the case is split, one worker taking the mother and one the child for treatment, colored sheets may be used but both are retained within a single folder. In the case of a sibling in treatment, another folder is usually made, cross-referenced by occasional notes. There is no point in making elaborate summaries for the related sibling folder. Workers should read *all* the appropriate material, whether on separate sheets or in separate folders, but this counsel of perfection is rarely followed either by psychiatrist or worker. If the sibling is not in individual treatment but remains part of the family treatment, it is better to use one folder with Volume II, if necessary, rather than cut apart essentially interpersonal material. It is a little easier to keep a single unit record

[7] R. R. Lee and M. E. Kenworthy, *Mental Hygiene and Social Work.*

in child guidance than in child placing, for reasons already noted. [8] The practices in child guidance and private family case work recording are today very similar, especially if psychiatric consultation is extensive.

Guidance records whether in a clinic setting or in a social agency doing family counseling and intensive treatment, tend to a good deal of diagnostic and evaluation summaries. Rorschach test results are also increasingly seen. Guidance (whether in clinic, or family, or children's agency), because the method of psychotherapy is chiefly that of interviewing, is reflected in narrative process style. Verbal and play behavior are fully observed and reported. Although increased skill in the use of relationship is making condensation by experienced workers feasible, because of technical discussions in seminars and individual consultations, more elaboration of detail has been encouraged than would be appropriate for some other types of case work service.

## · INSTITUTIONS

It is not possible to discuss the various types of court, "legal social," correctional and non-correctional institution records. Most have the common features of "team" products. Court records were once entirely adapted to the legal profession in terminology, format (legal-sized folders), and procedures. The movement is now in the direction, at least in domestic relations and children's divisions of the court, toward a legal-social focus, and a record which is midway between a family and clinic type record. Because of the basis of individual "offender," the court record is always individual or patient centered, with the family as "environment." Extreme variation locally as to court structure, function, staffing, and philosophy makes generalization difficult.

Children's institutions always have the classical problem of multiple departments, for example, school, cottage parents, case work, shop, recreation, and other activities. The ideal institution of the future will show a combination of case work and

[8] See p. 104

group work, educational, and other skills, in the living experience of the child; but the ideal case record, combining these skills, has yet to be developed. Group process records now being experimented with, combined with individual records, will prove very interesting. Meanwhile the trend here as in hospitals, is away from the departmental and toward the unit record. The problem of who is to contribute to and use the record has always been difficult since the role of the "aide" in the social work process (for example, foster parent, visiting housekeeper); or the fellow professional (for example, teacher, nurse) has never been so clearly distinguished as with the technician or fellow-professional in a medical institution. The case worker has had a natural and proper reluctance to exposing the record to untrained persons on the staff, with the added difficulty of confusion caused by so much individualistic contribution that the record loses unity by diffusion. There is no easy answer to this. Generally speaking, the aide, within which group we may include all varieties of substitute parents and many volunteers, does not contribute to or use the record directly, but reports to the case worker. The fellow professional, who is administratively part of the staff, usually has access to the record.

Institutions for adults use either the simple family case work type of record or, if correctionally or medically oriented, more psychological test and clinical material will be common, and the record conform to hospital usage. In all institutions if the central purpose—education for the school, medicine for the hospital, social work for the social agency—is conceded, the combining forces from the various professional disciplines can be harmoniously related in a unit record.[9] If a social institution is not regarded as such by the whole staff with social work purposes allowed to predominate, competition and confusion are bound to result.

Day care records for children represent a miniature edition of an "institutional" record, and some of the recording problems arise from the fact that the administrative person or matron is not always, nor is the staff always professionally trained. Granted

[9] See p. 12.

a day nursery with high standards, the record will contain: application data, with the reason for using the nursery made clear by the family situation, including emotional relationships and attitudes as well as family economics; health data, as prescribed by rules of the Board of Health; follow-up notes by the case worker on the child-family interaction, and follow-up notes by the teacher on the child's eating, dressing, play, sleeping, and other behavior while in the nursery. Habit and conduct disorders, whether noted in the family interviews or observed at the nursery, or both, should be discussed and recorded diagnostically in the record by the case worker. For convenience the face sheet may be a combination of application blank and eligibility (budget or fee charging) data. Health histories, on a standard blank, may be kept up by the nurse or other person. Records of required inocculations may be kept if desired on the registration card. This is a convenience if there are delays and changes of plan before actual entrance.

### · SHORT CONTACT AND BRIEF SERVICE

Since short contact calls for interviewing and other case work skills, the recording does not differ in principle from that of full length. The disciplines which have taught one to write a good short record are implicit in the disciplines of careful professional practice. All records are better for a lucid, brief style. All records should reflect the ability to focus the problem and clarify worker and client roles and responsibilities early. A long contact is not necessarily skillful, nor a short record a good record. Short records, like long ones, should have purpose, essential content, and a clear writing style. Short contacts include several variants: brief service cases in an agency with long-time functions; information and steering as in a referral bureau or center; and, brief services complete in themselves, as in an agency dealing with transients.

In the first variant—brief service, let us say in the family agency—a history sheet is started with or without a face card, with or without a manilla folder, depending on the seriousness of the service, the filing facilities, the probabilities of reopening, and office convenience. Brief services of this character may also be noted by medical or psychiatric social workers on the unit hospital chart without a formal work-up. With the referral center, if the service is one of routine information or steering only, no case record is made. A card file type of record with space for short notations is used. For the simplest sort of advice on where to go for services, an entry in a ledger or a tally count suffices. When correspondence is carried on, or other case papers kept, a supplementary folder will be needed. Many short-contact agencies use a double page folder, without cover, containing face sheet information on the upper half of the first page, followed by blank space for notes, the correspondence being inserted between the two pages. A printed outline of topics is not usually desirable, or if it is, a few pertinent headings will permit a sufficiently fluid write up along the lines of the agencies main concerns and responsibilities.

Short-contact cases are those intended to be short, focused to time-limited and treatment-limited services, completed usually in one dictation period. Such cases are common for aid to travelers and displaced persons in transit, selective service screening, communications in Red Cross, and many forms of counseling. Work with seamen is typically short-contact, though occasionally intermittent. Disaster and emergency conditions call for brief service and brief records. A short-contact agency may occasionally have a long-contact case, just as the reverse may be true. Contacts on continuing cases, infrequent or brief only because of heavy case loads, should not be regarded as short-contact. Nor should contacts broken by the client for his own reasons be so classified. The causes of such "brief service" should always be reviewed and studied very seriously.

Applications which result in non-acceptance are in a special category, and though short-contact, must be very carefully recorded in public assistance or similar agency. The basis for non-acceptance should be fully and accurately given. This holds true especially for the refusal of applications to board children, for public relations and fair hearings.

A short contact is focused usually to an immediate problem

and a specific service. A deep quality of relationship should not be stimulated, since it is to be terminated. A typical short contact will require a certain amount of practical factual material, but because a station desk is no place to encourage the giving of a life history nor to handle a deep transference this does not mean that attitudes and emotional overtones and discussion of the use of the service can be eliminated from the record. The dynamics of the interview focused to specific service and immediate action are just as important to record as in intensive therapy. Workers, however, should be cautioned against recording obvious procedures and small courtesies: "called the hotel and arranged for a room for Mrs. W. Took her across the street and said goodnight. She thanked me." "Bought a bus ticket." "Agreed to wire" (when by the time of dictation the return wire is already in the file). Instead, workers should notice and record in short contact, as in long, signs of composure or discomposure, independence, responsibility, or the reverse, protectiveness and anxiety. If we know how to interview about practical help we shall notice these emotional overtones, and we should be sure to record them. Failure to do this or to articulate the worker's role in the interview are the most characteristic faults. A short contact from the Army shows something of the interview process in this type of service:

JB, a 31-year-old "volunteer officer candidate," was referred to the Unit. His problem as stated was a desire for reclassification from Message Center School where he was experiencing dissatisfaction.

The soldier, a tall, soft-spoken, obviously intelligent person, approached his difficulty as a multiple problem. He had volunteered when the opportunity was offered to married men to present themselves for officers training with the proviso that they would have the privilege of relinquishing this status and returning to civilian life if they were not able to qualify. He had been in the army about six weeks, having completed the elementary stage of his basic training and had been assigned to specialized training. (Three months was to elapse prior to going to Officers Candidate School.) He expressed his present concern in several ways: his wife was ill with a chronic upper respiratory infection which had been aggravated by a visit to him while in camp; he was worried because her father died of Tb.

He was having difficulty keeping his mind on his work and was concerned about flunking out of the course, especially in view of the competition where he found himself surrounded by college men, while he only had two years of high school and four months of business school training. He talked at length about the complicated structure of the army and its administration. How being one of so many men made it difficult to know how to proceed. How civilians never could appreciate what was involved. He reviewed his own civilian progress in a success story from errand boy to manager of a meat market where he had been earning from $70 to $90 weekly, his marriage, his two children, his home, and his feeling of achievement. This brought him to his present predicament, in which the desire to "make good" in his situation and his fear of not being able to do so, his wife's present indisposition, the attitudes of civilians should he return not commissioned, and the complicated structure of the army all came into focus. Not knowing what to do next he had gone to the chaplain for advice. In that interview the chaplain thought a change of school assignment would be beneficial.

The problem was crystalized with the soldier around the question of his desire to "make good" in the Army. This was evidently shared by his wife, who had urged him to continue when he became upset about her illness. There was brief discussion of Tb. in which the soldier was given some information relative to the disease and where she could be referred. However, the main area of discussion centered around his present concern in relation to his army adjustment. The complexity of the Army, the need for Army experience (which he was just beginning to see and appreciate) in which he was a beginner. The possibility that perhaps these college men with whom he was competing were placing stress on their academic achievement (as he in the interview had on his own civilian accomplishments) because they, too, were finding this a new and complicated world in which to achieve a place or position. In this connection some of the requirements for Officers Candidate School were reviewed and some least common denominators such as minimum schooling, superior intelligence, army experience, "mature" judgment, a sense of responsibility, an evaluation by the board which had passed upon his candidacy and the stage of the game at which he found himself all became contingent. The soldier was able to derive a good deal of reassurance from his evaluation of himself in relation to the standards set and his own potentialities. The particular school in which he found himself offered valuable opportunity for learning army structure, administration and function, all of which were extremely important to OCS candidates. The interview closed with the soldier's withdrawing his request for reclassification and his asking for material which would enable him to prepare both for his present class and also for OCS. Suggestions were made in this direction and procedure for continued contact with the unit was indicated if he wished it.

### · SUMMARY

As regards public assistance records: money, income, assistance, is part of an individual's survival; it is as important as bodily and mental health, and to record economic or relief material calls for as much competence as can be brought to it. A person tends to react to the "relief" situation as he does to other life situations. Our handling of this material is often the focal point in the interview and in our relationship with the client. The "social component" in income is just as significant as the social component in medicine[10]—social services are as relevant, social work skills as highly developed, in the carrying out of the assistance program as any other, and these services and skills are appropriately reflected in the assistance record. Special needs relevant to the program, whether met or unmet, should be indicated. If there is a discrepancy between what we do and what we should do, this can be the basis for better staffing and social planning.

Public records must struggle against the tendency to unnecessary forms and inconvenient forms intended to standardize but serving only to encumber and stereotype. The format, structure and contents should be conducive to reading and use by the case work staff. The process style of recording should be used sparingly if at all; carefully prepared summaries and condensed narrative with *occasional* important interviews fully recorded make for a usable document. Case records are confidential; they are not "public documents," even though kept in a public agency. They must be professionally safeguarded in the public interest. Discussion of controversial issues must always be fully

[10]See Janet Thornton and Marjorie Knauth, *The Social Component in Medical Care.*

and accurately recorded, as must any departures from accepted procedure. This is a protection to both client and worker.

As regards child placing: So far as practicable, a unit record should be kept of parent, child, and foster home interaction. The good rule, one household, one folder, has to be qualified for the child placing agency, since in the foster home unrelated children may be placed. The rule remains, however, for the same family, one folder for own parents and siblings whenever possible. If siblings are placed in separate foster homes, more than one folder is usually kept. Whenever feasible administratively, especially within a single agency offering both the foster care and institutional care, let the record follow the child. Do not make duplicate records. In the separate folder kept of foster homes, after the initial work-up which shows personality and behavior through some verbatim (process) material, periodic summaries should be of a quality which permits condensation and subordination of evidence to the worker's judgment (evaluation). Primary evidence will be found through cross-reference to individual children's folders. This reduces undesirable duplication. The recording of non-acceptance of foster parents' application should be accurate and careful, are with most instances of non-acceptance.

Institutional records of all kinds are tending toward the unit or integrated type. Hospital records are always responsive to medical and psychiatric interest and call for careful gearing and condensation of social work aspects for "team" use. Psychiatric and medical social records show much greater similarity in content today than a few years ago, because psychosocial and psychosomatic interaction have become better understood. Child guidance records, while usually geared to the child as "patient," are more like a family agency record on the whole and, conversely, as family agencies engage in the direct treatment of children, the fields are less distinguishable, and the records are quite similar.

Children's institutions are social agencies, so that the various professional disciplines must combine toward a primary social work orientation and purpose. In general, only members of the professional staff contribute to and use a case record directly, but the team may include besides the social workers, nurses, educators, and others. The records for day care of children, comprising eligibility, family and social data, health and nursery observations, are also designed for team use, although the main responsibility for their contents is lodged with the social work staff. Information and steering centers typically work from a card or form, rather than a case folder, unless correspondence or other special functions are part of the regular set-up. Whenever referral centers begin regularly to keep case records, the inference may be drawn that they are turning into service agencies. Brief service cases in a family agency usually conform to the format of the "under care" case; in an agency carrying large numbers of brief service cases, as in work with transients, the format is likely to be a double page with printed face sheet headings.

The short-contact record is one intended to be short, time-limited, and focused to a specific service. Because practical, concrete services, or specific guidance are usually the object of the brief service or counseling, the emotional overtones of the interview and the worker's role, are too often minimized in the record. Mechanics and procedures, unless unusual, should be omitted, and more attention paid to the process of the interview. In short contacts resulting in non-acceptance of the application, careful recording of the reason for rejection is important.

# 9

## *LETTERS ARE AN IMPORTANT MEANS OF COMMUNICATION*

SOCIAL CASE WORK IS CARRIED ON THROUGH THE medium of oral and written communication. Letters play a strategic role in furthering direct service to the client, and in interpreting case work to the larger community. Direct service includes letters to the client and his family as a substitute for the personal interview; and inter-agency letters. Because the social problem typically has many facets—social work is conducted through a planned network of social agencies rather than through individual practice—letters have a rather unique importance. With all the attention given to formal methods of publicity we should never forget that each thoughtful and helpful letter written to an employer, an official, an interested friend, not only benefits the client, but widens the circle of those who understand something of the case work process. All letters to, from, and about clients, except for certain routine communications to be later noted, belong in the case record.

The rules for good letter writing don't change.[1] Don't write unnecessary letters; don't write until you have something to say; don't put your correspondent to unnecessary trouble; be careful about names and titles of your correspondent and identifying data for your client; whenever possible, obtain the consent of your client before writing on his behalf; be prepared to exchange only pertinent information of common interest and concern, that is, don't tell your correspondent what is none of his business,

[1] Mary E. Richmond, *Social Diagnosis*, Chapter XVII, p. 317. Mary Richmond wrote beautiful letters herself, and taught something of the art to anyone willing to learn. See also Margaret C. Bristol, *Handbook on Social Case Recording*, pps. 132–167, for concrete suggestions.

or ask him for what is none of yours; and finally, remember the old adage—what well may be thought, cannot wisely be said, and what quite easily may be said face to face must often be said very carefully in a letter if, indeed, it can be written at all.

### · *LETTERS TO CLIENTS AND THEIR FAMILIES*

These fall into two main types: letters which are a substitute for the personal interview, and routine letters and notifications. Letters to clients serve the immediate case work purpose for which they are written, and do not conform to any pattern. They should be geared to the relationship and the client's understanding both in content and style; and they should establish a link to former or projected contacts. Beyond this, little generalization is applicable. In all letters to clients we should consider the facilities for receiving mail, the exposed tenement-house box, the rural post office, the curiosities which may be aroused by unwonted correspondence. Plain, rather than agency envelopes may be tactful, unless the client has indicated otherwise. In short, one should respect the client's cultural habits and use one's imagination constructively. Stereotyped letters to relatives whom one does not know, asking them to assist a person, usually have little effect. Scolding and cajoling are no more persuasive in a letter than in an interview, which is to say, not at all. Persuasion rests on adequately motivating the correspondent, which is a highly individual thing.

Routine letters and notifications, such as appointments given, do not deserve filing, and a carbon copy merely adds unnecessary bulk, strains fastenings, and retains something of no permanent value.[2] A note in the daybook or other office reference showing that an appointment or other communication has been sent is sufficient. If repeated appointment letters are ignored, or significant appointment behavior comes to the surface, then an entry in the text will be appropriate. Occasionally an appointment letter contains some genuine "treatment" elements (not to be confused with ordinary small courtesies) and so the usual carbon would be kept.

[2]See also p. 16.

· *INTER-AGENCY CORRESPONDENCE*

If agencies are housed in the same building, or personal communication is easy, conferences and telephone calls may take the place of many letters. Letters, however, are more to be depended on for accurate reference, are sometimes timesaving to both parties, and are essential for long distance enquiry and reporting. Both ethical and practical considerations make letter writing a serious discipline. To say merely that we are interested in a case is to give the other agency no real point of intersection, whereas, if we state the problem and *what we are doing about it,* this can be immediately joined with the correspondent's purposes. The first observation made by any reader is that many letters should not have been written at all. There are occasions when putative fathers or deserting husbands or the parents of runaway children have to be communicated with through a third party, and there are emergencies of every kind which justify a hasty letter while one is attempting to understand the situation with which one is confronted. But in general we should caution ourselves to be sure that one's own course of action is clear before a letter is undertaken. Nor should we ask another agency to gather information which with a little more time and skill we could elicit from the client himself.

As between two professional agencies we may assume that the problem itself is sufficiently stimulating, and that social agencies do not need to be cajoled or urged to cooperate if the inquiry lies in the appropriate area. But if the mission is difficult, the distance great, or the agency unused to the service requested, the writer will do well to consider the ordinary frailties of human nature and supply the correspondent with a reasonable interest motivation and add such courtesies as make the service easier. The State Hospital which once wrote to a family agency somewhat as follows had not only an inadequate sense of professional function, but very little knowledge of human nature:

Dear Madam: John Smith, a patient in our hospital, left a straw suitcase at 16 West Colorado Street, and also left a brown overcoat with large lapels in the Grand Union Terminal. Please forward both to us and we will gladly pay the expenses.

A more persuasive though informal letter, written to a rural county superintendent, reads, in part:

For the last few days I have been trying to run down the parentage of the above-named child, Buster Berrien, but thus far I have not heard from my inquiries. However, I still have hope!

Mrs. Martin, the boarding mother, thought the child was diseased, but I had a blood test made and just yesterday the report came in saying it was negative. A urinalysis was also made, and this was reported negative, but for some reason or other the child is very much undernourished and is exceptionally thin and anemic. He seems bright and normal mentally. This morning I went to Dr. Wilson's office and talked with him about the child. He suggests that the chap be placed in the Radcliffe Hospital under his care for a month or two to see what can be done to build him up. Dr. Wilson will give his services, but the hospital bill will be an item, of course. If the child could only get built up, I have no doubt but that he would be very placeable in a foster home; but as it is, his future is dubious.

Would you permit me to place him in the hospital as a county charge for a while, to see how he develops, or would you care to make some other suggestions?

Aside from the rather obvious attempt to induce this official to underwrite an unwelcome expense, note the tact of the concluding question. Too many writers tell the correspondent what to do, rather than ask for suggestions. Too many writers assume an attitude of private ownership.

Early letters of inquiry were a recapitulation of most of the facts in the case, often followed by a long list of specific questions which would have been less necessary if the writer had taken pains to explain his own role and interest:

We are interested in Ruth Red, age 19, an unmarried mother, living at 338 Forbes Avenue. Her former home was in Y and her parents are dead. (A paragraph of history follows.) May we ask for verification of the girl's story, and will you telegraph us, collect, the result of your investigation. We particularly wish to know (1) who paid for her fare from P to W last April, (2) whether the Burns Davis family are willing to receive her and, (3) what Burns says about the question of paternity, etc., etc.

Quite commonly, as in the letter above, few clues were given as to the nature of the service already instituted. From every point of view, professional courtesy and common sense, one owes the correspondent the reason for writing. The most usual as well as the most persuasive reason lies in having reached some point in treatment which calls for the good offices of another agency. It is this point of shared concern and shared service, which makes the letter pertinent to each. It is always important to give a clear interpretation of one's own plan of treatment. Letters are often used to confirm a telephone conversation.

The medical social field was one of the first to attempt a real interpretation of the medical social role:

Mr. John Smith, Director            January 11, 1935
Public Welfare Department         Re: Emil S—
—————————————          No. 44988–A
—————————————          2638 Monte Ave.

My dear Mr. . . .

As you know, Mr. S. was in the hospital from December 6 to December 18 for a hernia operation. This was not performed because of patient's heart condition, which is due to high blood pressure. When he reported to Cardiac Clinic on January 9 he complained of headaches and his blood pressure was still rather high. The doctor ordered an electrocardiogram, which was taken on January 10, and which showed some recent changes in the coronary arteries, which may interfere somewhat with the blood supply to the heart.

It is therefore imperative at this time that the patient have complete bed rest for a period of two weeks and avoid all worry and excitement. Arrangements have been made for a visiting nurse to call in the home daily, and patient is to return to clinic on January 31, at which time another heart test will be taken and patient will be again seen in Cardiac Clinic. We have communicated with the family regarding these recommendations.

We would appreciate hearing from you regarding patient's sleeping arrangements, facilities for rest and care in the home, and any social treatment you are arranging. May we have this report before his return appointment, if possible?

Sincerely yours,

                        Director of Social Service

Or this, to a vocational service agency. Note the focusing to the probable area of shared concern:

My dear Miss R.

I am sending you a summary of our contact with the above boy about whom I spoke to you last Thursday, December 13th.

John has been treated at this hospital since 1939 for scleroderma. This disease is characterized by his hand being short and stubby, blue color, and his knuckles, elbows, and other joints ulcerating. Reacts to cold, should wear extra warm clothing, gloves, etc., and will always have to protect himself against the cold. In spite of deformity of his hands, John has showed a marked ability in working with his hands, designing and carving small airplanes, boats, etc., and working with radios and electricity.

John left school last year after finishing the grades. Although he did not do brilliant work, he was a fair student, well-liked, dependable and industrious, according to a report from the principal of P.S. 11 in the Bronx. He left school because the family had been forced to move continually, and because he had lost a great deal of time as a result of illness.

Since social service has known the family they have had a hard time financially. The father is unemployed and the mother has tried to secure day's work to help out. At present the family are receiving assistance in New Jersey, and Mrs. F. is having a difficult time managing to secure the high calcium and vitamin special diet that John needs. However, the whole family are devoted to the patient, who is a quiet likeable boy, very thorough and industrious.

He is most interested in learning a trade in which he could use his hands. Some of our doctors have suggested toy making, and we shall be very interested to hear of your recommendations. I have told John that you will send him an appointment, and I have asked him to bring some of his work for you to see.

Sincerely,

Social Worker

On the same case, the material was arranged somewhat differently for a public assistance agency thus (an extract):

John has a vascular disease known as scleroderma. This is manifest by extreme tightening of the skin and feet with callosities at the knuckles, elbows, and joints. John's condition is a chronic one, but we are hoping to give him some relief. He should not be subjected to cold weather, should live in a warm apartment, wear warm clothing, hose, gloves, etc. He has been treated with pancreas medication and injections (supplied by social service) and he has now been placed on a high calcium and high vitamin diet. He should have the following diet daily: one large helping of meat, one and a half quarts of milk, one egg, two ounces of cheese, one and a half cups tomato juice, two oranges, three vegetables, one salad, two fruits.

Our dietitian has estimated that this diet should cost about $.42 to $.45 a day above the regular Home Relief budget in New York. Bread, butter, potato, cereal and rice have been estimated at $.12 to $.15 daily. John, who has been on this diet since November 13, 1934, when last seen on November 27th, had gained seven pounds. Mrs. F. has tried to secure it for the boy, but because of financial troubles, has found it difficult. The doctor states that it is too soon to evaluate the actual benefit of this diet to John's physical condition. . . .

We would greatly appreciate hearing from you in reference to your plans for the family. We have been somewhat disturbed about the family's ability to secure John's diet. Since we do not have a copy of your budget, we are not sure whether the relief to John's family is to cover his diet, or whether this could be supplemented at our doctor's request.

Such attempts to focus the correspondence to mutual problems are replacing the older types of overall reports.

A letter written during the depression years from a voluntary to a public assistance agency shows weighting towards the economic circumstances:

Mr. John Doe, Director
Public Welfare Agency
————————————————
————————————————

April 1, 1934
Re: (Identifying data)

My dear . . .

The C. family were first known to us on 3/15/33, when Mrs. C. applied for financial assistance. At that time Mr. C. had been out of work eight or nine months, and Mrs. C., five or six months. Relief has been given on a weekly basis since that time. Mr. C. has had only two days' work during a year's contact with the family. Mrs. C. has been doing part-time domestic work off and on. Relief has been varied each week, according to the C.'s income; so that a minimum budget of $12 ($5.25 rent, $5.45 food, $1.20 carfare) has been covered. Clothing in kind has also been given when the C.'s have expressed a need for it. Total relief during this period has been $451.65.

Mr. C. is now receiving treatment from the City Hospital Skin Clinic. Apparently most of the financial responsibility for the family has been shouldered by Mrs. C. for some time, and she has expressed resentment over Mr. C.'s inactivity. She has often said that if he were working, things would be all right. Mr. C. said that he is anxious to work but has been unable to find employment. He feels that his relationship with a private organization has kept him from getting a city job. He has been employed as a porter in the past. Mrs. C. has done part-time domestic work. Among her more recent employers are: (Identifying data omitted.) These references have been verified and the work history found satisfactory.

The marital situation seems to be aggravated at times by Iris' presence in the home. Since Iris is not Mr. C.'s child, Mrs. C. often says that he has no right to discipline her. Mr. C. says that he is as interested in Iris as if she were his own. Our interviews with Iris have indicated that she is not fond of Mr. C. Mrs. C. has told us that Iris will do nothing Mr. C. tells her, and Mr. C. says that Iris is completely disobedient and will not even obey her mother. Efforts have been made by us to help the C.'s towards a better understanding of themselves and their situation. Recreational facilities for Iris have been discussed, and Iris has joined the Girl Scouts and the YWCA. She is going away to camp for two weeks from June 26 to July 11.

We would like to refer this family to you for maintenance or possibly for cooperative care. Will you let us know when it would be convenient to have a conference?

Yours very sincerely,

District Secretary

In the foregoing, note that Agency A is careful not to repeat a medical diagnosis but to give a clue to the area of difficulty for Agency B's guidance.

While the practice of sending very full case histories is yielding to selection of material, there are many occasions when full summaries should be sent to cooperating agencies. Between agencies with regular working arrangements carbon copies of the social study are sometimes made for referral, but it is more usual to prepare a summary for the particular purpose to be served. Reports for clinic or similar study follow a pattern outline described earlier.[3] A good report, like a good letter, gives the reason for referral. This reason is the incident or chain of events leading to the present reason for referral. Thus we say:

After three years of intensive supervision of Flora in her mother's home, the breakdown and commitment of Mrs. C. to State Hospital has meant that we must make immediate arrangements for this girl to live away from home. We are, therefore, sending Flora to you to talk over the possibility of Girl's House, etc. etc.

We do not begin:

In March 1940 Mrs. C. was referred to us for family assistance and guidance. At that time Mr. C. had again deserted, leaving Mrs. C. with Bill, age 19, who was somewhat grudgingly supporting his mother, Tom (a long account of Tom and what we did about him here), and Flora, then a girl of 13.

All this history may well be supplied, but Agency B will grasp the situation much more readily if the incident which precipitated referral is given first, and the rest of the history subordinated to the central points of treatment intersection between the two agencies now sharing the case.

In requesting an out-of-town agency to undertake a difficult mission, more circumstantial data are required than in cases in which the person himself has been the client of both agencies. The more delicate the interview, the more detail the correspondent will probably need. A clear picture not only of the present situation and treatment proposed by Agency A for itself, but of attitudes and history, will be of great help in preparing the correspondent. In intimate matters, however, one should remember, especially if one's correspondent is not a professional person but a village postmaster, that the letter may be read aloud to relatives or a former employer. The word "Confidential" in red written across the top of the letter does not necessarily insure protection, and the letter itself must have such dignity, simplicity, and restraint as to give the least possible

[3]See p. 47.

cause for offense. Technical language, dubious at best, should be rigidly excluded.

In correspondence between agencies conducting a large amount of shared routine "business" the steering blank has proved useful. Public welfare departments communicating with public schools, or family and medical social agencies exchanging current information may find the blank adequate for simple factual reports. The content of the blank is that of a skeleton letter with identifying data, reason for referring problem, treatment as carried on by Agency A, and a request, either general or specific, of Agency B. If the case is difficult, subtle, or unusual, the blank will not suffice, and a letter should be substituted.

## Etiquette

It is hardly necessary to mention that all letters should give the exact name and title of the addressee and the proper identification of the case. For family agencies the mode of identification is usually the same as in social service exchange clearings, (names, including unmarried name, and ages of all members of the immediate family), but in writing to agencies like hospitals or courts which may keep a "patient" instead of a family index it is as well to give the patient's name on a separate line and underline it. In addition, one should add such administrative identification as may be known, namely, clinic number, ward, court designation, which will help in record searching. Letters should never be patronizing in style or seem to withhold information because the correspondent is not able to understand. One should give only necessary and relevant information to any correspondent. Confidential reports and diagnoses given by Agency A to Agency B should not be passed on to Agency C without general or specific permission to forward such communications. In writing about a client's religion, one should be careful to avoid phrases which might be offensive to the correspondent. This does not happen often, but astonishing tactlessness is occasionally found. The oft-repeated advice is still good—when one is angry at another agency either don't write the letter at all, or write it and read it over in a day or two before mailing. This will tend to mellower public relations. As a matter of tact and common sense, one should not use the terminology of another profession in writing to a psychiatrist, physician, or judge. Then is the time to write most, not least, like a social worker. Any diagnosis made should be a social work, not medical or legal, opinion.

Letters to agencies are usually signed by the executive or designated supervisory personnel. This fixes agency responsibility, safeguards agency agreements, and helps to channelize information for the use of staff. Often very important policies by implication are worked out in letters, and careful office routing, therefore, is essential. Case workers change more often than executives, and the continuity of signature makes community relationships clearer. This does not mean that executives should assume professional responsibilities which belong to the case workers. The name of the person dictating the letter should be found in the lower left hand corner and the correspondent will then use the "attention of" device in reply. While this may seem over-meticulous, nothing is really gained if the administrative function is confused. Workers are not in private practice, and department heads and senior workers have certain responsibilities for interpretation of policy. There are always exceptions, as in rural districts and with small staffs, in which each person may be very well known in the community. But with large urban staffs of young workers and students, established procedures for letters and signatures reduce mistakes and are a protection for everyone. Letters to clients are signed by the worker in his own name, and hand-written ones are sometimes appreciated.

· *SUMMARY*

Letters should be carefully timed to serve an effective purpose. Letters to clients may serve as a substitute for a personal interview, and require great care in their preparation. Appointments—original letters or carbons—should not usually be kept. With inter-agency correspondence the consent of the client should usually be obtained before inquiring or reporting about him. We should transmit or request only such information as is relevant to the shared professional purpose. We should not put correspondents to unnecessary trouble to find out something which, with a little time and patience, one could discover oneself. In making a request of any agency which does not know the client, enough data should be given to make the service possible, but so far as possible reports should be considerate of both the client's and the other agency's interests, economical and well focused to the necessary shared concerns. Agencies asking for information should be prepared to give an account of their own thinking and planning. This is the justification and reason for asking. Asking for information always assumes a reciprocal obligation. Care should be exercised in the small accepted courtesies and conventions of correspondence—address, identification, style, and signature. Good letter writing is one of those agency habits which can make an important contribution to public relations.

# 10

## *CONCLUSION*

GOOD RECORDING MUST REFLECT A GOOD LEVEL OF practice. Social case work today is concerned not only with meeting basic human needs, as in programs of social security and public welfare, but with many other aspects of socialized living. Records are for use—to furnish accurate reference on case details and equally, through self-supervision, staff discussion and research, to improve individual skill and the general quality of service. The record describes the nature of the difficulty, the causes of these difficulties, the eligibility status; it formulates the diagnostic picture, and explains the role of the worker in services of practical helpfulness, reduction of strain, counseling, guidance, and social therapy. The social case worker operates in the field of interpersonal, especially interfamilial, relationships, from his own special angle and with his own special contribution. The case worker and the group worker as well, must observe human behavior and social interaction with informed understanding, and he must be able to translate the most elusive of all human experience, namely, feeling, into the record. This is shown chiefly through the interviewing process, including play interviews with children.

The record, however, is not the case; it is a way of describing and telling the meaning of the case. While a plain style is always best, the skilled recorder does not rely on faithful reproduction of events, behavior, and interviewing contents alone, but he should condense, select, formulate, and interpret trends through diagnosis and evaluation. Whenever new contents are being assimilated in practice, recording tends to overelaboration in those areas until the implications are more fully grasped and mastered and, therewith, simplicity achieved. Case work, like all professional disciplines, is compounded of science and art. With its scientific part it must continually search for unities and principles, and with its art it must be always more closely and deeply responsive to individual uniqueness. In an ultimate sense only the trained diagnostician can write a good record, for only he can pluck from the unending web of social experience the thread of probable significance.

# BIBLIOGRAPHY

Abramson, Eva, The Supervisor's Job in the Public Agency: Administrative Aspects. Chicago, American Public Welfare Association, 1940.

American Public Welfare Association, Recording and Reporting with Regard to Old Age Assistance under the Social Security Act. Chicago, 1935.

Breckinridge, S. P., Medical Social Case Records. Chicago, University of Chicago Press, 1928.

Bristol, Margaret C., Handbook on Social Case Recording. 2d ed. Chicago, University of Chicago Press, 1937.

Browning, Grace A., Rural Public Welfare; Selected Records. Chicago, University of Chicago Press, 1941.

Bruno, Frank J., "Some Case Work Recording Limitations of Verbatim Reporting," *Journal of Social Forces*, Vol. VI, No. 4, June, 1928.

Burgess, Ernest, What Social Records Should Contain to Be Useful for Sociological Interpretation. *Journal of Social Forces*, Vol. VI, June, 1928.

Cannon, M. A., and P. Klein, Social Case Work, New York, Columbia University Press, 1933.

Chase, Stuart A., "Can Interviews be Described Objectively?" *Journal of Social Forces*, Vol. VII, No. 4, June, 1929.

Clark, Mary A., Recording and Reporting for Child Guidance Clinics. New York, Commonwealth Fund, Division of Publications, 1930.

Cockerill, E. E., "Psychiatric Understanding in Case Work with Surgical Patients," *The Family*, February, 1943.

Corscaden, James Albert, History Taking and Recording. New York, Hoeber, 1926.

Dixon, E. S., and Grace A. Browning, Social Case Records; Family Welfare. Chicago, University of Chicago Press, 1938.

Eliot, Thomas D., "Objectivity and Subjectivity in the Case Record," *Journal of Social Forces*, Vol. VI, No. 4, June, 1928.

Family Welfare Association of America, Report of Recording Committee, Milwaukee, September, 1934.

Finck, George H., "Establishing Routines and Procedures," *The Family*, March, 1936.

Fisk, H. I., Statistical Recording and Reporting in Family Welfare Agencies. New York, Family Welfare Association of America, 1934.

Gartland, Ruth M., Psychiatric Social Service in a Children's Hospital, Chicago, University of Chicago Press, 1937. The University of Chicago Social Service Monographs.

Hall, Beatrice, "The Social Service Record in the Unit Medical History," *Hospital Social Service Magazine*, Vol. XX, No. 1, July, 1929.

Hamilton, Gordon, A Medical Social Terminology. New York, Presbyterian Hospital, 1930.

—— "Notes on Current Practices in Medical Social Case Recording," *The Family*, Vol. XII, No. 3, May, 1931.

Hollis, Florence, Social Case Work in Practice, Six Case Studies. New York, Family Welfare Association of America, 1940.

Houwink, Eda, "An Experiment in Recording," *The Family*, February, 1936.

Isaacs, Susan, Social Development in Young Children. New York, Harcourt, Brace and Co., 1933.

Journal of Social Work Process: Vol. I. The Relation of Function to Process in Social Case Work, 1937; Vol. II. Method and Skill in Public Assistance, 1938; Vol. III. Social Case Work with Children, 1939; A Functional Approach to Family Case Work, 1944. Pennsylvania School of Social Work, University of Pennsylvania.

Judge Baker Foundation, Case Studies. Boston, The Foundation, 1922. Series No. 1.

Lee, P. R., and M. E. Kenworthy, Mental Hygiene and Social Work. New York, Commonwealth Fund, Division of Publications, 1929.

Lewis, Helen Baum, "Case Work Notebook," *Social Work Today*, April, 1941.

Lundberg, George A., "Case Work and the Statistical Method," *Journal of Social Forces*, Vol. V, No. 1, September, 1926.

—— Social Research; a Study in Methods of Gathering Data. New York, Longmans, Green & Co., 1929.

MacIver, R. M., Social Causation. New York, Ginn & Co., 1942.

Maeder, LeRoy, "Diagnostic Criteria; the Concept of Normal and Abnormal," *The Family*, October, 1941.

Pray, Kenneth L. M., "The Place of Social Case Work in the Treatment of Delinquency," *The Social Service Review*, vol. XIX, No. 2, June, 1945.

Queen, Stuart A., Elements of Record Keeping for Child-helping Organizations, New York. New York, Survey Associates, 1915.

Reynolds, Bertha E., "Between Client and Community," *Smith College Studies in Social Work*, Vol. V, No. 1, September, 1934.

Richmond, Mary E., Social Diagnosis, New York, Russell Sage Foundation, 1917.

—— "Why Case Records?" *The Family*, November, 1925.

Robinson, Virginia P., "Analysis of Processes in the Records of Family Case Working Agencies," *The Family*, July, 1921.

—— A Changing Psychology in Social Case Work. Chapel Hill, N. C., University of North Carolina Press, 1934.

Rogers, Carl R. Counseling and Psychotherapy. Boston, Houghton, Mifflin, 1942.

Sheffield, Ada E., Social Case History; Its Construction and Content. New York, Russell Sage Foundation, 1920.

—— "The Situation As the Unit of Social Case Study," *Social Forces*, Vol. IX, No. 4, June, 1928.

Slavson, S. R., Introduction to Group Therapy, New York, Commonwealth Fund, 1943.

Social Case Histories of Public Assistance Agencies. Social Security Board, Bureau Circular No. 8, March, 1939.

Southard, E. E., and M. Jarrett, The Kingdom of Evils. New York, Macmillan, 1922.

Swift, Linton B., "Can the Sociologist and the Social Worker Agree on the Content of Case Records?" *Journal of Social Forces*, Vol. VI, No. 4. June, 1928.

Taft, Jessie, The Dynamics of Therapy in a Controlled Relationship. New York, Macmillan, 1933.

—— A Functional Approach to Family Case Work. Philadelphia, University of Pennsylvania Press, 1944.

Tennant, Gertrude, "Prize Medical Social Case Record," *Social Service Review*, Vol. I, No. 3, September, 1927.

Thornton, Janet, and Marjorie Knauth, The Social Component in Medical Care. New York, Columbia University Press, 1937.

Towle, Charlotte, Social Case Records from Psychiatric Clinics; with Discussion Notes. Chicago, University of Chicago Press, 1941.

U. S. Children's Bureau, Publication No. 101: Office Administration for Organizations Supervising the Health of Mothers, Infants and Children of Pre-School Age, by Estelle B. Hunter. "Planning Case Record Systems," pp. 52–70; "Statistics," pp. 70–76; and "Record Filing," pp. 77–91. Washington, 1922.

—— Publication No. 171, The Work of Child-Placing Agencies. "Recording the Successes and Failures of Foster Homes," pp. 49–50, Washington, 1927.

—— Publication No. 269, "Recording Child Welfare Services," Washington, 1941.

Waller, Willard, "Insight and Scientific Method," *American Journal of Sociology*, Vol. XI, No. 3, November, 1934.

Weed, Margaret, "Recent Changes in Record Writing," *The Family*, May, 1932.

White, Helen V., "Recording, a Dynamic in Case Work," *The Family*, October, 1943.

Young, Erle F., "Scientific Study of Social Case Records," *Journal of Applied Sociology*, Vol. IX, No. 4, March-April, 1925.

—— Provisional Manual of Directions for the American Council. Revised from *Educational Record Supplement*, No. 8, July, 1928.

· *REFERENCES ON THE CONFIDENTIAL NATURE OF THE CASE RECORD*

American Association of Social Workers, Committee on Records, Washington, D. C. Chapter, The Confidentiality of the Agency-Client Relationship. March 15, 1943.

Castendyck, Elsa, and Anne F. Fenlason, "The Confidential Nature of Social Case Records in Public Relief Agencies," *The Family*, February, 1936.

Family Welfare Association of America, Safeguarding the Confidential Nature of Case Records in Public Agencies. January, 1940.

Federal Security Agency, Social Security Board. Bulletin to State Agencies Administering Approved Public Assistance Plans: "Standards for Safeguarding Information Concerning Applicants and Recipients of Public Assistance."

Hamilton, Gordon, Theory and Practice of Social Case Work. New York, Columbia University Press, 1940, pp. 341–343.

Merriam, Ida C., "The Protection and Use of Information Obtained under the Social Security Act," *Social Security Bulletin*, Vol. 4, No. 5, May, 1941, pp. 13–19.

Resnick, Reuben B., and Harry Graham Balter, "Withholding Information from Law Enforcement Bodies," *Social Service Review*, Vol. VIII, No. 4, December, 1934, pp. 668–677.

Welfare Council of New York City, Committee on Confidential Use of Records of the Family Service Section. Manual of Practice in Relation to Use of Confidential Agency Records. March, 1943.

Wigmore, John Henry, Evidence. 3d ed. Boston, Little, Brown and Company, 1940, Vol. 8, Secs. 2285 *et seq.*

· *REFERENCES ON HOW TO WRITE*

Fowler, H. W. and F. T., The King's English. New York, Oxford University Press, 1922.

Graves, Robert, and Allen Hodges, Reader over Your Shoulder, New York, Macmillan, 1943.

Kierzek, John M., The Macmillan Handbook of English. New York, Macmillan, 1939.

# INDEX